Medieval Pedagogical Writings

AN EPITOME

Sarah B. Lynch

kısmet·press

Libera Scientia | Free Knowledge

Medieval Pedagogical Writings: An Epitome
by Sarah B. Lynch

Epitomes, 3
Series Editors: Tim Barnwell & N. Kıvılcım Yavuz

Published in 2018
by Kismet Press LLP
15 Queen Square, Leeds, LS2 8AJ, UK
kismet.press
kismet@kismet.press

Copyright © 2018 Sarah B. Lynch

Published by Kismet Press LLP under an exclusive license to publish. Commercial copying, hiring, lending is prohibited. The book is freely available online at <kismet.press> under a Creative Commons Attribution-NonCommercial-NoDerivatives 4.0 International (CC BY-NC-ND 4.0) license. See <https://creativecommons.org/licenses/by-nc-nd/4.0/> for details.

Downloadable .epub edition also available

Printed and bound by IngramSpark with acid-free paper, using a print-on-demand model with printers in the US, EU, and Australia

A catalogue record for this book is available from the British Library

ISBN 978-1-912801-00-8 (pbk)
ISBN 978-1-912801-01-5 (ebk)

Contents

Introduction	1
I Authors and Works	9
II The Beginning and End of Elementary and Grammar Education	43
III Organising the School Day and Schoolroom	51
IV Corporal Punishment	63
V Natural Ability	77
VI Morals and Religion	87
VII Being a Teacher	105
VIII Education of Women	115
Conclusion	129
Notes	131
Bibliography	145

For Ruth

Acknowledgements

As a younger scholar, I can't in any way thank everyone who has helped with my work. Too many friends, colleagues, and teachers have read drafts, been patient sounding boards, and (most critically) understood my never-ending need for tea.

To Christine Meek and Rosalind Brown-Grant for introducing me to some of the works around which this book revolves. And to Robert Black and William Flynn for supervising my doctorate.

To the Institute for Historical Research (London), the Sir Richard Stapley Educational Trust, and the Royal Historical Society for their financial assistance. These awards helped me get to the libraries and archives that I needed and made me feel like I was on the right track. And to the Wall Street Institute of English, Lyon, and its previous director, Pierre Colliot, for giving me a job that helped me stay in Lyon for an extraordinary two years.

To Tim Barnwell, N. Kıvılcım Yavuz, and Ricky Broome at Kısmet Press for all their hard work on this project and especially to Tim for his patience during a difficult year. We need more publishing endeavours like

Kısmet focused on open access publishing in academia. I wish everyone involved the very best.

To the denizens of the Le Pat and the MAH.

To Mark Lewis Tizzoni, for being there. And finally to my parents, Patrick and Frances, who have tirelessly supported me throughout the years. Thank you.

Introduction

What Are Medieval Pedagogical Writings?

WHAT ARE MEDIEVAL PEDAGOGICAL WRITINGS? The simple answer is that they comprise of any work that deals with the nature of learning and teaching and how these activities should be carried out. That neat description functions quite well for most of this little book but it falls down if we ask it other questions, such as what did 'medieval pedagogical writings' look like? What kind of template did they follow? Were all the authors who wrote medieval pedagogical works teachers? Can they be placed into one category that predisposed them to write about medieval education? The complex truth is this: medieval pedagogical writings didn't all look the same, they didn't follow a particular template, or address the very same topics or questions. This one here is a systematic treatise on education but that one is a letter, that other one a poem. Some only discuss education in a small subsection of a much larger work, perhaps on the subject of reviving the Crusade. Medieval pedagogical advice was written by people in very disparate positions, many of whom were not teachers in any shape or form, and some of whom had no obvious business writing about education. This is why this *Epitome* is not called *Medieval Educational Treatises*, because then could we really look at Bernard of Chartres's classroom practice, as recorded by a man who had never met him and certainly never been taught by him? Could we justify examining a poem of the allegorical four ages of man or a set of rules drawn up for choirboys? Perhaps, but perhaps not.

Medieval pedagogical writings defy classification. They struggle with being a discreet genre because they don't take the same form or style, spilling across the boundaries from poetry to didactic tracts to epistles. Only their common subject matter lends them consistency. In this guise, they could be a subgenre of prescriptive literature but even that is awkward because their tone is not always demanding and regulating but occasionally contemplative. They engage with everyday questions of teaching and learning, seeking to modulate the black and white of their advice with areas of grey. One of the most interesting examples of this in pedagogical writings is the sensitivity to individual circumstances, from the natural gifts of the individual pupil to the challenges faced by the individual teacher.

This *Epitome*, therefore, does not discuss every single piece of writing on education read and composed during the Middle Ages. Alas, it cannot. Instead, it concentrates on themes revisited by a selection of antique and medieval authors (from the first century to the fifteenth). These themes can be found in other works that discuss education in the Middle Ages. This is the principal aim of this book: to provide a framework of interrogation that can be used far beyond the texts examined here.

Why Read Medieval Pedagogical Writings?

The whole history of medieval education — from elementary education right the way to the university — has been greatly helped by the existence of a large number of works dealing with pedagogy. While these works express the personal experiences and opinions of individual authors, they also provide information on common forms of educational organisation, as well as showing what topics were of most concern to medieval people. Pedagogical literature, therefore, allows the modern person to glimpse the ideas that surrounded elementary and grammar education in the later Middle Ages. In addition to revealing theoretical frameworks for schooling below the level of the university, they attempt to engage in the realities of medieval education too. Yes, many medieval commentators on instruction wanted to imbue the whole experience with Christian morals but how did one do that? How did one put the theory into effect? From Jerome to Pope Pius II, they all offered justifications and recommendations that were seen as feasible, advice that could be employed within the real classroom.

Works such as the ones discussed here also allow us to listen into the medieval educational debate. Just as pundits today go back and forth on class sizes and the importance of early childhood education, these writers wrote arguments and counterarguments on aspects of pedagogy as diverse as whether girls should be instructed or whether masters should beat their pupils. And these were debates that ranged over centuries. Furthermore, the evidence provided by literature on education can be directly compared to that emerging from documentary sources, like proceedings of church chapters and municipal councils, and teaching contracts. There is much agreement between the theory and what is revealed in these medieval documents: for example, there is abundant proof that shows that the age of seven really was the usual age to begin formal education and wasn't just an arbitrary age set down by commentators. But sometimes they didn't agree. Many of the authors focused on the intangible benefits of moral and spiritual betterment of Christian instruction, but many parents who sent their children to school were not immediately concerned with the saving power of reading the Bible in Latin. While the religious aspect would have pleased them, they were equally interested in the more tangible social and economic benefits. The dreaded spectre of return-on-investment haunted medieval parents and teachers too.

So we get can get a lot out of medieval pedagogical writings. We can explore the ideas that (some) people had about elementary and grammar education, as seen above. But we can also get some more concrete information about what schooling was like in the Middle Ages. Philippe Ariès wrote in 1960 that 'it is difficult for modern man to visualise' premodern education without examining 'the conditions of life in the school and its environment'.[1] Happily, many historians since then have rectified that deficiency (see the recommendations for further reading at the end) but he did hit upon a problem we all face when looking into the past. How do we reconstruct it in order to *see* it and, even more importantly, what materials can and should we use? In the case of medieval elementary and grammar education, we have many sources but the treatises and poems and letters that we look at here give us more than the fees pupils paid or the size of the building the master rented. They give us the feel of education, the atmosphere in which it took place. We know that corporal punishment took place but these works help us understand why. It was not merely the relationship between a *bad* action and a *punitive* reaction but a wide-ranging interplay between questions of discipline and purification. There was also an intense awareness of the cause and effect of corporal punishment, with theorists openly discussing the dangers of producing damaging levels of shame and, ultimately, anger in the pupil. Medieval pedagogical writings, therefore, give us a distinctive impression of what actual instruction was like, for teacher and for pupil. Indeed, the information available in these works provides the backdrop, the painted scene, before which the facts of medieval education perform. They recreate the mental milieu in which teachers and pupils operated, usually unconsciously, but they also seek to describe in more elevated terms the instruction of children, which could be treated with contempt in the Middle Ages.

The final reason why we should read and examine the medieval pedagogical writings is that the production of such manuals and so on demonstrate that elementary and grammar education was considered worthy of such attention. Elementary and grammar education was where children learned the fundamentals of literacy of the Middle Ages: how to read, how to say their prayers, how to understand Latin (the lingua franca of the educated), how to write, and how to compose correctly. Many pupils would have only participated in the first, most elementary, part of this instruction, learning their prayers and how to sound out the written word and perhaps how to write their name (a useful talent in the later Middle Ages when an increasingly legal-minded society required witnesses). Those who advanced into more explicit grammar education might have ended up reading Terence and Seneca and other authors studied at a university level. Despite its elementary nature, several of the great minds of the Middle Ages spent time considering this category of education. Jerome wrote about how a little girl's hand should be clasped in her teacher's in order to show her how to hold a stylus. A German graduate of the University of Paris deliberated upon how the perfect schoolhouse should be built. Jean Gerson, preeminent theologian of his time and Chancellor of the University of Paris, grappled with how best to teach the basics of faith to little boys and girls. It didn't matter how basic this education was; what mattered was that it was fundamental to all other academic endeavours. It laid the foundations for all intellectual activities and the authors of the works discussed here recognised that fact, and made elementary and grammar education a fitting subject for theoretical debate. We are often tricked into thinking that the Middle Ages was somehow anti-knowledge, indifferent to learning or, at least, dismissive to all else but pure theology. Medieval pedagogical writings belie this assertion, exploring as they do the most rudimentary levels of instruction in many different manifestations.

A Brief Note on Terminology

Since this *Epitome* is principally concerned with what is written about elementary and grammar education, we should consider that term and what exactly it seeks to describe. There were no national education systems in the Middle Ages and, as we will discuss in Chapters 2 and 5, there was no firmly designated age when a child was supposed to be learning a specific subject or engaging with a subject at a predetermined level. Elementary and grammar instruction, and the schools and teachers who offered it, principally meant any formalised education that was taking place below the level of the university. It could be utilised as preparation in order to enter a university but it could also stand alone, acting as training for other trajectories in life, from becoming a skilled craftsman to making a good marriage. It was primarily a conduit for acquiring Latin literacy. In later periods, it also offered instruction in writing, arithmetic, and even in vernacular languages. Elementary and grammar education was usually experienced by those who were quite young, usually between the ages of seven and fourteen. Then again, as we will see, it was never restricted to that age group, with younger children attending schools and older teenagers continuing much later as need and opportunity allowed. The term 'elementary and grammar education', in other words, is exactly that, a period of instruction in which the fundamentals of literacy and other academic subjects were introduced to primarily children.

I
Authors and Works

THIS IS A VERY SHORT INTRODUCTION TO EDUCATIONAL treatises read and written in the Middle Ages up to 1500. It is not, in any way, a definitive list, or even a 'best of' list. Instead, this *Epitome* highlights some widely-read works (by Quintilian, Augustine, Jerome), some little-known works (the *Commendation of the Clerk*), and some very curious works (Pierre Dubois's *Recovery of the Holy Land*). So what works are we going to look at in this little book? Which writers spent the time writing about education and specifically elementary and grammar education?

Quintilian

The Education of an Orator (*Institutio oratoria*),
ca. 95, Latin

Marcus Fabius Quintilianus (ca. 35–ca. 100) was a noted rhetorician of the first century, who was probably from Hispania. Educated at Rome, he appears to have returned home to Hispania to practise law, only returning to Rome as a very low-level member of the entourage of the emperor Galba in 69. His lack of importance was probably what saved him after Galba's assassination and he did not actively participate in politics after this point. Instead, he opened what became a well-regarded school in Rome. There he taught rhetoric, the art of discourse and debate, to the sons of the Roman elites, including Pliny the Younger (serial letter writer and witness to the eruption of Vesuvius). Tacitus may also have been a student. The emperor Vespasian (69–79) made Quintilian a consul. As a result of the extra income from this appointment, he was able to concentrate more on his school rather than on pleading cases.

Quintilian wrote *The Education of an Orator* in his retirement from teaching and the law, and it became the handbook for the study and practice of rhetoric. Rhetoric was one of the key skills needed by educated Romans in order to engage fully and successfully in public life. Indeed, Quintilian himself described the goal of his instruction as producing an active citizen and decried those who withdrew from the public arena:

> I would not have my orator a philosopher, since no other group of men has withdrawn farther from the duties of citizenship and from all the tasks of oratory.[2]

The Education of an Orator is made up of ten books, almost all of which are dedicated to an in-depth analysis of the rules of rhetoric, the stringent requirements for speaking and writing well. Book I, however, is what we are interested in here, as it goes into the mechanics of early education. While Quintilian was not the first to write about this level of education (he mentions the work of Chrysippus), his work became the foundation of all later pedagogical writing, from Jerome to Aeneas Silvius Piccolomini. This widespread influence belies the traditional transmission of *The Education of the Orator*. It was supposedly lost in its entirety until it was 'rediscovered' in the monastic library of Saint Gall in Switzerland in 1418.[3] It is clear that sections of *The Education of an Orator*, especially Book I on elementary and grammar education, were available at least as early as the twelfth century. John of Salisbury had access to Book I at Chartres when he was writing his *Metalogicon* in the middle of the twelfth century and Vincent of Beauvais quoted heavily from Book I when he was writing during the thirteenth century. We cannot be certain if John and Vincent were working from coherent sections of the text or whether they were using a selection of quotes from Quintilian (known as *florilegia*), but we can be certain that they and others saw Quintilian as the ultimate authority on educational advice. Even though he was a classical writer, he was very much the keystone of medieval educational theory.

Quintilian examined many of the issues faced by teachers throughout history. While *The Education of an Orator* was a textbook for aspiring politicians, lawyers, and bureaucrats, it was also a handbook for teaching. In Book I, Quintilian distilled his years of experience and created a way to discuss the practice of teaching and learning. What he discussed is what everyone discussed (and sometimes still discusses). He looked at the effects of parents and the household on the future abilities of children (which continues to be a particularly ripe source of discussion amongst my friends who are teachers and classroom assistants). He discussed when the best time to begin formal instruction was. He looked at how the atmosphere of the classroom, and the actions of teachers and pupils, affected teaching and learning. He deliberated upon the use of corporal punishment, setting up a millennia-long debate on violence in the classroom. He examined the challenges of teaching in a mixed-ability classroom. Almost every pedagogical source of disagreement is found within Quintilian. He is the authority who articulated the concept of early education.

Augustine

Confessions (*Confessiones*), 397–98, Latin
On Christian Doctrine (*De doctrina Christiana*), 397–426, Latin

While Quintilian gives us the vocabulary and structure in order to discuss elementary and grammar education, it is Augustine of Hippo (354–430) who gave oratorical and rhetorical skills a second incarnation as essentials for Christian life. Augustine the man almost needs no introduction. Born in the Roman province of Numidia in North Africa (modern-day Algeria) to a devoutly Christian mother and a pagan father, he was educated close to home in the classical Roman style and later went to Carthage for further studies. He later taught Latin grammar and rhetoric in his home town, in Carthage, and then in Rome and Milan. It was at Milan, influenced by another great orator, Ambrose, where Augustine converted to Christianity.

Augustine is important to the study of educational writing for two reasons. Firstly, he gave an extraordinarily frank account of his own instruction as a young child in the autobiography of his conversion, his *Confessions*. Here we find a first-person description of the experience of a classical education. He showed that, for his father, the expense of schooling was meant to lead to an elevated economic and social status. He also described the terror of corporal punishment and his failure to acquire a level of fluency in Greek as a result of a brutal master. Then again, it was events in his boyhood that convinced the older Augustine that there was an inherent evil even in children that required chastisement and physical correction. When it came to bodily suffering, including corporal punishment, Augustine's approach was certainly conflicted.

Augustine's second influence on educational writing was his promotion of traditional Roman grammatical and rhetorical education as being appropriate for the burgeoning Christian community. Still struggling to reconcile Christian beliefs and their position as the favoured religion of the state, Augustine's *On Christian Doctrine* and other works provided a map towards being a Christian and being an educated Roman. One of the most important outcomes of classical education was the ability of the student to then partake fully in the public life of the state, to enter onto the *cursus honorum*, or the 'course of offices'. But what was the use of such training if, as a Christian, you were supposed to reject worldly things? If, as a devout believer, you were going to sell your family estates and live in a monastic community (as Augustine himself did at one time)? Augustine advocated continued study of grammar and rhetoric not to prepare to be an active citizen of the Empire but instead to become an active citizen of heaven. Grammar allowed the Christian to better understand the Holy Scriptures. Rhetoric allowed the Christian to preach the Word more effectively and to win over doubters with subtle debate. As Augustine put it, reading Cicero's now lost work *Hortensius*:

> changed the whole feeling of my mind, giving a new direction to the prayers I offered to You, O God.[4]

Augustine's advocacy was essential for the continued importance that grammar and rhetoric played in medieval education.

Jerome

Letter to Laeta, 403, Latin
Letter to Pacatula, 413, Latin

Jerome (ca. 347–420), Augustine's contemporary and fellow Church Father, was another brilliant student of classical learning who turned to an ascetic Christian life. Born in Illyria (modern-day Croatia), little is known about his own education before he moved to Rome as a teenager. There, he studied under Aelius Donatus, composer of the *Ars grammatica* (*The Art of Grammar*), one of the most popular textbooks on Latin grammar in the Middle Ages. Jerome was torn between his love of secular learning and his desire to devote himself utterly to his Christianity, which he fully embraced as a student in Rome. For a period, he rejected all classical literature and focused solely on the Bible. And it is for his translation and edition of the Bible that he is best known.

Jerome, however, did not confine his activities to the Bible. He was a prolific writer of treatises (against Christian heresies such as Pelagianism) and of letters, two of which are discussed here. Jerome acted as a personal spiritual advisor to many friends and associates over his long life but his relationship with high-ranking Roman women revealed much of his more practical guidance. The women he corresponded with were from prominent, usually patrician families, and they often reciprocated with spiritual, emotional, and financial support. And it was to women such as these that Jerome directed letters on the education of their family members.

The best known of these is Jerome's letter to Laeta. Laeta was the daughter-in-law of Paula, Jerome's most generous patron, and the mother of Paula the Younger, the subject of Jerome's letter. This communication contained a remarkable course of study for little Paula as it recommends an entirely 'Christian' education. The little girl was to have exposure only to Holy Scripture and the works of appropriate theologians, such as Hilary of Arles. Her first readings were to be taken from the Psalms. She was to be completely sheltered from worldly things. This may seem extreme but it must be remembered that the little girl's grandmother and mother had already decided that she would enter the monastic life. Jerome's educational plan was specifically tailored for this purpose. Indeed, it appears that Jerome rejected the classical tradition in which he himself was educated. This, however, is not true and the influence of Quintilian is everywhere. Jerome directly paraphrases Quintilian's discussion on the importance of educated and involved mothers in the educational process, and uses the same ancient examples, Cornelia Africana (d. ca. 100 BCE) and Hortensia (fl. ca. 42 BCE). Jerome advises that Paula be given cut-out letters to play with as does Quintilian. They only differ because Jerome mentions that they can be made of boxwood or ivory while Quintilian only mentions ivory letters. Both Jerome and Quintilian recommended that a tablet incised with the alphabet be made and that the child would trace the letter with a stylus to practise forming the shapes. Jerome may have rebelled against the classical world, he may have seen the works of Scripture as being the only writing really worth reading, but he still advanced the pedagogical methods of Quintilian. Augustine may have theorised that classical instruction was valuable as a means to an end, but it was Jerome who actively embraced the methods of classical instruction.

Ælfric Bata

Colloquies, 11th century, Latin

Little is known about Ælfric Bata, a Latin teacher and writer in pre-Conquest England. He identified himself as a student of the noted grammarian and homilist, Ælfric of Eynsham (d. ca. 1015), and his own work indicates his intellectual descent from the tradition of Anglo-Saxon colloquies. He also identified himself as a 'small monk' and, considering the rowdy tone of his Latin grammar text, gives us the impression of a raucous character. This is reinforced by another reference to him in the *Miracles of Saint Dunstan* by Osbern, where the saint has to intervene from above in order to prevent Ælfric Bata relieving the monastery of Christ Church Canterbury of some property.[5]

What we do know is that Ælfric Bata wrote an intriguing textbook aimed at the young oblates in an Anglo-Saxon monastery. He himself was the teacher and the work was probably something he wrote and used with his pupils. (This is reinforced by the fact that two of the three surviving manuscripts appear to have revisions and additions in his own hand.) It consists of conversations in Latin between oblates and masters and between oblates and oblates, ranging from the very basics to quotations from Scripture and patristic texts. These *Colloquies*, however, are far from boring interactions between masters and pupils. The extraordinary vulgarity and violence portrayed in the text, along with less-than-exemplary Latin, has divided scholars. It is unclear if Ælfric Bata was simply reflecting a 'monastery gone wrong' or whether he was using extreme, even comedic language to entertain (and thus successfully teach) his pupils.[6] In many ways, the atmosphere reflected in the *Colloquies* is much more reminiscent of the chaos of the fictional St Trinian's and St Custard's (full of mad romps and casual relationships to literacy) rather than the calm, disciplined educational experiences of little Paula and Pacatula.[7]

The *Colloquies* are of interest to us here as they contain enormous amounts of information on the daily lives and instruction of young boys in an Anglo-Saxon monastery, from what the boys were supposed to wear (listed in the form of complaint in Colloquy 26) to what sort of transgressions merited corporal punishment (a multitude!).

Hugh of Saint-Victor

Didascalicon (*On the Study of Reading*), after 1120, Latin[8]

Hugh of Saint-Victor (*circa* 1096–1141) was a long way removed from Augustine and Jerome, yet he grappled with the same questions regarding a Christian education. Hugh's background is very obscure but he was either Saxon or had Saxon connections, and he is associated with a priory in Saxony. Around 1120, he moved to the abbey of Saint-Victor near Paris in order to study and eventually became head of the abbey's school.

These were heady times, when the schools in and around Paris became the focus of extraordinary intellectual activity. Hugh's work, the *Didascalicon* or *De studio legendi* (*On the Study of Reading*) was written in this atmosphere. It was a deeply philosophical work that principally discussed how learning was not only a way to understand Scripture better but a saving activity in and of itself. Being instructed in the liberal arts was, according to Hugh, a path to salvation. In this he was clearly influenced by Augustine. Unsurprisingly, the *Didascalicon* did not dwell on elementary and grammar education but rather on promoting a religious tone. The concept that the instruction itself was a religious activity (though not entirely original) fed into later medieval approaches to schooling. Hugh also had some intriguing views on natural ability that demonstrated the awareness many medieval authors had of the individual characteristics of pupils and students.

John of Salisbury

Metalogicon (*On the Arts of Verbal Reasoning*), ca. 1159, Latin

The *Metalogicon* was a theoretic consideration of the subjects of grammar, logic, and rhetoric by John of Salisbury (ca. 1120–80). Like Hugh, John's background is unknown but it appears that he was of Anglo-Saxon, not Norman extraction. We know nothing of his early education and it is unlikely that he was either rich or connected. He went to Paris as a teenager, where he studied briefly under the notorious Peter Abelard and then moved to the cathedral school at Chartres, also in northern France. In these places, he studied not only Scripture and theology but also the great works of antiquity that were available at that time. And it is at Chartres that John formed the idea of the perfect teacher.

The *Metalogicon* is a fascinating work that promoted the value of a liberal education in grammar, rhetoric, and logic. Indeed, Daniel D. McGarry's 1955 edition of the text is subtitled a 'Defense of the Verbal and Logical Arts of the Trivium'. During the twelfth-century rage for all things philosophical, John did not want the fundamentals to be forgotten and gave ample justification for their continued study and importance. What is particularly of interest to us, however, is the *vignette* of Bernard, a grammar teacher from Chartres, which John provided in the midst of this treatise. John had never met Bernard of Chartres, who had died shortly after John was born, but his pedagogical methods were still being used at Chartres, and stories of his teaching practice lingered decades after. John presented Bernard as the perfect master, 'the greatest font of literary learning in Gaul in recent times'.[9] And he proceeded to explain exactly how Bernard approached each sentence of Latin read in the classroom, what grammatical exercises he gave his pupils and students, how he punished wrongdoing (specifically plagiarism). So, in the middle of his theoretical arguments for the importance of liberal education, he slipped in a case study of actual teaching techniques, available to be followed by the eager teacher. It cannot be argued that the *Metalogicon* was a handbook, but the section on Bernard of Chartres is a reminder that it was not meant as a pure intellectual exercise either. John expected his readers to take note of what he wrote and, perhaps, follow the pattern laid down by his ideal master.

Pseudo-Boethius

On the Teaching of School (De disciplina scolarium), ca. 1230–40, Latin

De disciplina scolarium was a wildly popular work on education. Probably written in Paris, it experienced almost immediate success. Nothing is known about the actual writer except — based on a remark within the text — they were associated with the University of Paris, and that they were possibly from Northern or Eastern Europe.[10] Vincent of Beauvais (see below) freely quoted from it and copies were produced from England to Bohemia — Olga Weijers identified at least 111 copies in collections across Europe and North America. It represents a relatively early example of the dedicated treatise on education, a genre that was in the process of emerging in the thirteenth century. Its intended audience was probably professional educators and others interested in the process of learning. One manuscript from the fifteenth century (now in Munich) was copied by 'Johannes Schürbrand of Laugingen, rector of the school in Weilhaim'; in other words, by the local schoolmaster in a small Bavarian town. Another, earlier manuscript appears to have been prepared in Italy for the humanist poet, Petrarch.[11]

The work itself is wide in its scope, ranging from the subjects that should be covered, to different capabilities amongst pupils, to how one becomes a schoolmaster.

One of the distinct problems with *On the Teaching of School* is that it does not state explicitly if it is aimed at the education of younger children, older children covering grammar, or even advanced students of philosophy and theology. Instead, it touches on grammar, dialectics, as well as elementary instruction. Furthermore, it is particularly interesting in its discussion of the training and comportment of teachers, a practical discussion that was usually ignored by other works with the exception of the *Commendation of the Clerk*. No doubt the Pseudo-Boethian text was an inspiration for the later author.

Vincent of Beauvais

On the Education of Noble Children (*De eruditione filiorum nobilium*), before 1249, Latin

Vincent of Beauvais (ca. 1190–ca. 1264) was one of the most widely-read authors of the later Middle Ages. His biography is murky, like many of our authors. We know nothing of his childhood and education, and the only facts that we do have is that he was a Dominican friar and that he spent the latter part of his life as reader at the Cistercian abbey of Royaumont, just outside Paris. We also know that he had an intellectual association with the French royal court and that his opus major, the *Speculum maius* or 'The Great Mirror', was promoted and patronised by the court. Vincent's *Speculum* was intended to be a compendium of all knowledge, from astronomy and astrology to military tactics to a history of the world. Even more impressive than the scope of the work was how it demonstrated Vincent's own knowledge, especially his familiarity with classical and medieval authors, as well as authors in Arabic. This was a man who sought to know everything and transmit this to the wider public. The historical part of the *Speculum maius* (adventurously entitled the *Speculum historiale*) was, for want of a better word, a bestseller of the later Middle Ages, both in the Latin original and in translations into the vernaculars of Europe, such as Jean de Vignay's translation into Middle French in the 1330s.

Unsurprisingly, with his encyclopaedic knowledge, Vincent became a favourite of the French royal family. He acted as a kind of educational consultant to Louis IX of France (who was canonised in 1297) and his wife, Margaret of Provence. He did not teach the royal children but he did offer advice directly to the king and queen, in the form of letters and in the form of a treatise on education. *On the Education of Noble Children* was a substantial addition to the literature on education in the Middle Ages. It not only discussed the theory and tone of the instruction of aristocratic boys and girls, but also the practicalities of such instruction. Vincent was deeply influenced by both Quintilian and Jerome too, not only in approaching education in a practical manner but in directly quoting Quintilian and Jerome. Indeed, this is another reason why Vincent's work is so valuable. Because of his heavy use of quotes and his constant appeals to the authority of previous authors, we can see what kinds of books were available to someone interested in education in the thirteenth century. While Vincent was a special case (Louis IX was actively acquiring books on his behalf), *On the Education of Noble Children* still demonstrated that there was an awareness of practical pedagogy as a discreet subject and that there was access to pertinent information on it. Finally, *On the Education of Noble Children* set aside work on education from that increasingly popular genre, mirrors for princes, which tended to meditate on broader considerations such as the ideal traits of rulers and concepts of the state. Vincent's advice would have been quickly disseminated through court circles, eager to copy the royal couple's household as a matter of fashion and as a matter of advancing their (and their children's) prospects. While Hugh of Saint-Victor framed his recommendations in a clerical context, Vincent of Beauvais was writing for the secular nobility. Once again, the *cursus honorum* was open and an educational framework was needed to tread upon that path.

Philippe of Navarre

The Four Ages of Man (*Les Quatre ages de L'Homme*), ca. 1270, French

Philippe of Navarre or Novara (ca. 1200–ca. 1270) was not a religious like Vincent of Beauvais or Hugh of Saint-Victor. Instead, he was a servant of the Ibelin family from the Kingdom of Jerusalem. He was a kind of jack-of-all-trades, doing administrative work for the family, up to and including serving as a diplomat on their behalf. He was a warrior and a writer, composing a chronicle of the Ibelin's dispute with the Holy Roman Emperor, Frederick II (who claimed the Kingdom of Jerusalem). He also appears to have had some legal knowledge as he also wrote a treatise on feudal law. It is of interest to note that he primarily wrote in French, though he himself hailed from the region around Novara in Northern Italy. French was widely spoken amongst crusaders in the Holy Land and had become a new lingua franca in noble and knightly circles.

Philippe's poem, *The Four Ages of Man* (*Les Quatre ages de L'Homme*), was a moralising treatise on the four ages of man: childhood, youth, middle age, and old age. This was a very popular literary and artistic trope in the Middle Ages, and it examined the different aspects of each 'age'; what one should expect and what one should do. The first two ages, childhood and youth, were concerned most with preparing for life. And Philippe did indeed comment on how children should be educated. His focus was on gaining a decent level of literacy and on cultivating a strong faith. He discussed knightly instruction and he also discussed clerical instruction, and emphasised the way that a career in the Church could raise a poor boy from poverty to wealth and power. His advice, therefore, matched the milieu in which he existed. Education was important not necessarily as a means of pursuing abstract knowledge but as a way of acquiring worldly skills and advancement. This focus was imperative in the crusader states where strength and cultural uniformity had to be maintained in the face of Muslim pressure and European interference. Philippe's advice was sharp and opinionated, especially on the instruction of women, who he felt should almost never be educated at all.

Giles of Rome

On the Direction of Princes (*De regimine principum*), ca. 1278, Latin

Giles of Rome (ca. 1243–1316) was very much Vincent of Beauvais's successor as educational consultant to the French royal family. Hailing from Rome — though likely not a member of the noble Colonna family as once claimed — he became both prior general of the Augustinian Friars and bishop of Bourges. A student of Thomas Aquinas, he was a noted Aristotelian theologian who had been caught up in a backlash against the popularity of Aristotle's philosophy at one time. However, the successes of his later career and the fact that he was declared *doctor beatus et fundatissimus* 'blessed and best-grounded doctor' by Benedict XIV in the eighteenth century shows that this controversy was short-lived. He had a similar connection with Philip III of France as Vincent of Beauvais had with Philip's father, Louis IX, and was clearly favoured by his advisee, Philip IV 'the Fair'.

On the Direction of Princes is a work that sits comfortably into the genre of 'mirrors for princes'. It provided the standard information thought necessary for future rulers, including lengthy exhortations on the importance of being a moral king or prince. Since the body of the ruler was a microcosm of the body of the state, an avatar even, the training and the conduct of the future ruler would have direct implications for the state. And education was one of the subjects dealt with by Giles. He focused on three aspects of education: religious instruction, the subjects that were to be taught, and the nature and characteristics of the teacher. He discussed in depth the importance of religious education for children who were not intended for careers in the Church and he emphasised the acquisition of Latin. As the language of scholarly learning and the lingua franca of Western Europe, it was a necessary accomplishment. Learning it also promoted diligence and other fine virtues. Not all rulers during this period had the level of Latin that Giles promoted.

On the Direction of Princes was widely read, especially after it was translated into French around 1330. Its title in this manifestation, *Li Livres du gouvernement des rois* or 'The Book of the Government of Kings' clearly indicated its intended role as handbook for good government. The object of Giles's advice, Philip the Fair, did not appear to take much of the guidance to heart. Philip was, after all, the French king who helped destabilise the Papacy, which lead eventually to the Western Schism in 1378. He also expelled the Jews from his kingdom and suppressed the Knights Templar. But it should also be noted that, as bishop of Bourges, Giles was present at the council that denounced the Templars.

Pierre Dubois

On the Recovery of the Holy Land (*De recuperatione Terrae Sanctae*), 1305–07, Latin

While Philippe of Navarre wrote for the Latin community in the Holy Land, Pierre Dubois (fl. ca. 1300) was writing about creating an entire community whose sole purpose was to crusade and to crusade successfully. Dubois was a royal *advocat* in Constances, Normandy, around the turn of the fourteenth century. He appears to have attended the University of Paris for a time — where he heard lectures from Thomas Aquinas and Sigur of Brabant. Well-schooled in scholastic philosophy and methodology, it is also likely that he studied at the University of Orleans, just south of Paris, which was a centre of civil legal studies. He himself does not appear to have had any particular links to the Holy Land but it is clear that he was strongly affected by the fall of Acre in 1291, as was most of Christendom. The capitulation of the last crusader city in the Holy Land and the removal of the kings of Jerusalem to Cyprus had resulted in many calls for a renewed crusader spirit in Europe. Pierre Dubois's 'plan', however, reached much further than simple rhetoric.

On the Recovery of the Holy Land was a statement outlining a radical retooling of European, and specifically, French society in order to create a culture whose sole goal was the successful recovery of the Holy Land. And for Dubois, this had to begin in childhood. Children, both boys and girls, would be selected at the age of five and sent to schools where they would train in every conceivable subject, from philosophy and theology to engineering, from medicine to languages, from the art and practice of war to carpentry. What Dubois was proposing was not only a military conquest but a cultural and religious conquest, using men and women trained in these schools to bring a Christian Holy Land to fruition not through force alone, but through leadership and persuasion.

The hearts and minds of the inhabitants were the true objective. While *On the Recovery of the Holy Land* survives in only one manuscript (Vatican, BAV, Reg. Lat. 1642), it reveals that some saw education as the means to reinvent late medieval society, that education was the 'silver bullet' for the ills of Christendom. Dubois's theories and recommendations were indeed drastic and it is unlikely that they came to the attention of his master, Philip the Fair of France. After all, Dubois had advocated that the property of the recently-condemned Templars should be used to finance these schools. This same property had just been confiscated by Philip.

Geoffrey de la Tour Landry

Book for the Education of his Daughters (*Livre pour l'enseignement de ses filles*), ca. 1370, French

Geoffrey de la Tour Landry (ca. 1320–91?) was a nobleman from Anjou in France who saw some action in the Hundred Years' War against England. He served at several sieges and battles between the 1340s and 1370s as a company leader. Nothing is known of his education except that he certainly was well-read in French, and possibly also in Latin. He himself owned a collection of works including the Bible and chronicles of France, Greece, and England, and so on.

The *Book for the Education of his Daughters*, written around 1370, was composed by Geoffrey for his three daughters. While it concentrated on moral topics, it underlined the necessity of providing formal instruction to daughters and other female dependents. For Geoffrey, an educated woman, a woman who had learned to read and who had studied Scripture and other appropriate writings, was someone who could effect change and prevent injustice. A woman who was educated could also better retain her own honour. He gave the example of a lady called Delbora, who was well-educated and a person to whom people came for counsel. Her husband was a cruel and evil man but, because of her own learning, she was able to mollify him and ensure that he treated his people well. A literate woman was, therefore, an asset. This approach directly opposes Philippe of Navarre's horror of educated women, with the terrible possibility that women might be able exchange letters with lovers. While Geoffrey did not insist on teaching women to write, he felt that women should be able to take their place in the world as well-informed and morally-trained participants.

The *Book for the Education of his Daughters* had an extraordinarily successful afterlife. Written originally in French, it was widely read in aristocratic circles. Unlike Pierre Dubois's *On the Recovery of the Holy Land*, Geoffrey de la Tour Landry's work is preserved in at least twenty-one medieval manuscripts. It was translated into English twice in the fifteenth century, including by William Caxton who printed his English edition in 1484. It was also translated into German as *Der Ritter vom Turn* and printed in Basel in 1493. An edition history like this indicates The *Book for the Education of his Daughters* was in demand by the noble and bourgeois book buyers who drove manuscript and early-printed book production in the later Middle Ages.

Anonymous

The Commendation of the Clerk (*De commendatione cleri*), 1347–65, Latin

We have looked at many authors so far whose personal biographies are lacking in detail. The author of *The Commendation of the Clerk*, however, is completely anonymous. This treatise appeared in Lynn Thorndike's rather wonderful *University Records and Life in the Middle Ages* in 1944, a collection of source documents that revealed the everyday experiences of life in medieval universities. Working from a single known manuscript (Vatican, BAV, Pal. Lat. 1252), Thorndike suggested that the author was a German cleric who attended the University of Paris. It is easy to suppose, then, that the anonymous author received an education very similar to what he described in his *Commendation*.

The treatise belongs in a subsection of educational literature directed at boys who were preparing for clerical orders. Guillaume de Tournai's early-thirteenth-century *On the Instruction of Boys* (*De institutione puerorum*) also provided advice for the same type of pupil, boys from non-elite backgrounds who were attending schooling for the expressed purpose of becoming clergy. Both are directly influenced by Pseudo-Boethius's *On the Teaching of School*. The *Commendation of the Clerk* is very entertainingly written, and represented the further growth of interest in the practical methods of providing elementary and grammar education. Its focus on the mundane aspects of instruction revealed information on how pupils were viewed as individuals and on how a teacher could tailor their approach in order to teach efficiently each boy under their tutelage. In some ways, this treatise marked a return to discussion of 'normal' classroom teaching that Quintilian considered in his work. Neither Quintilian nor his much later German colleague taught in the exclusive atmosphere of a royal or noble court. And while Quintilian was indeed teaching Roman elites, he was doing so in a group context and with a specific goal in mind, the training of public men. The anonymous author of the *Commendation* also discussed larger-group teaching with a similarly explicit goal, the training of clerics. Furthermore, the anonymous author, like Quintilian, clearly had real-life experience as a pupil and as a teacher, and his advice is original, direct, and relatively unencumbered with quotes.

Jean Gerson

For the Boys of the Church of Paris (*Pro pueris ecclesiae Parisiensis*), ca. 1400, Latin
A.B.C. for Simple People (*A.B.C. des simples gens*), ca. 1401, French
To the Tutor of the Dauphin (*Au précepteur du Dauphin*), 1417, Latin

Jean Gerson (1363–1429) was the kind of boy that Philippe de Navarre was writing about when he said that through education, 'the son of a poor man can become a great prelate'.[12] While perhaps not destitute, he came from a peasant background in the Ardennes region of northern

France. Again, we know nothing of his education. We do know, however, that his family was intensely religious, and that three of his brothers became Celestine monks, while four of his sisters followed a religious life within their own home. We also know that his village, the village of Gerson, was owned by the abbey of Saint-Remy at Rheims and it is likely that an intelligent boy (whose parents were happy to spare him) could attend school and catch the eye of the local ecclesiastical authorities. At fourteen, the typical age to begin university-level studies in the fourteenth century, he arrived at the Collège de Navarre at Paris. This was the starting point of a brilliant career as a theologian, a writer, and eventually Chancellor of the University of Paris. He was deeply involved in the theological and ecclesiastical affairs of the time, including his campaign to resolve the Papal Schism. He presided over the Council of Constance (1414–18) and its condemnation of Jan Hus. On top of all of this, he condemned Jean Petit's notorious attempts to justify the murder of the Duke of Orleans by the Burgundian party and thus brought the displeasure of John the Fearless, Duke of Burgundy. Gerson eventually withdrew from public life and, after a few years in exile, lived out the last decade of his life at the church of Saint-Paul in Lyon.

Gerson was a prolific writer on the subject of education. Not only did he write a lot about education, he also wrote about it in so many different ways. He wrote letters and statutes for schools. He wrote poems and proverbs.[13] He wrote weighty treatises and simplified catechisms. And he wrote both in Latin and in French, intending that his texts should reach the maximum number of readers.

Gerson's pedagogical works are impressive because they provide insight into several types of medieval education. His 'charter' for the choirboys at the cathedral of Notre Dame at Paris provided detailed information on what such children learned and how they were cared for. His letter to the Dauphin's tutor describes the instruction he felt was required for a future king, and included a detailed list of books that he should read. Additionally, he did not neglect those on the lower end of the social scale with his works on elementary education in the vernacular, and addressed his 'catechism' to all the boys and girls, and all the people, both great and little in the eyes of society. Like the anonymous author of the *Commendation of the Clerk*, he wrote clearly and simply. Rather than relying on quotations and florilegia, he sought to engage his readers directly and not merely overwhelm them with evidence of his intellect. He played many roles within his works. He acted as an educational consultant to the Dauphin (much like Vincent of Beauvais and Giles of Rome), writing to his tutor but never engaging with the pupil himself. He created practical guides for the instruction of future clerics, in the same vein as the anonymous German author and Guillaume de Tournai. But he also was the religious pedagogue, crafting accessible lessons on faith for an increasingly literate society.

While we know Gerson would have conducted classes at the University of Paris, he was best known as an advocate for the University and its administrator. For example, he was made Chancellor at the age of thirty-two, only three years after he received his doctorate in theology. His writings clearly demonstrate, however, that he had a strong interest in pedagogy and in elementary pedagogy at that. This interest is probably the basis of an unsubstantiated claim regarding his time in Lyon. Many biographers have asserted that, at the collegial church of Saint-Paul, he held a school for local children in his retirement, teaching them elementary literacy and the articles of faith. Unfortunately, there is no firm evidence from archival sources, and even in his obituary (recorded by his colleagues at Saint-Paul), he was described as Chancellor of the University of Paris and preeminent theologian. On the other hand, we cannot rule out such activity. There was, at the very least, a school for choirboys at Saint-Paul, and it is not impossible to imagine that Gerson may have enjoyed engaging with these pupils.[14] For the time being, without any conclusive documentary evidence, such a claim must remain a theory.

Aeneas Silvius Piccolomini (Pius II)

On the Education of Boys (*De liberorum educatione*), 1450, Latin

Aeneas Silvius Piccolomini (1405–64) is probably the author about whom we know most, in terms of the kind of man he was. He wrote an autobiography, his *Commentaries*, which not only describes much of his life but is a rare first-person account by a reigning pope. Piccolomini was another example of a poorer boy 'made good', not through a life's career in the Church but through the practice of humane letters. He was born into a noble family in a village in the territory of Siena. His father had been brought up at the ducal court of Milan but bad luck and the seizure of aristocratic assets by the government of Siena effectively left his family in penury. He helped his father work the land and he played with village children so his childhood was not unlike that of a fifteenth-century peasant. Nevertheless, he still had an edge over his peers in the village. His parents were literate so his father in particular was able to teach him. He also received some instruction from the local priest. Piccolomini's break, however, was when he was eighteen. His aunt lived in Siena and had enough wealth to offer her nephew room and board in order to allow him to attend university at Siena. This was four years later than most students began their university careers: for example, as mentioned above Jean Gerson entered the university at Paris at fourteen.[15] Piccolomini had to do some serious catching-up and studied relentlessly in order to do so, including nearly burning himself to death when he fell asleep over his books one night. He eventually became a teacher in Siena and Florence, and a writer. His most famous work was a saucy epistolary novel in Latin, *The History of the Two Lovers*, which was very popular in the fifteenth century. He then became secretary to a number of senior churchmen and the Council of Basel (which ran from 1431 to 1449), and eventually entered the service of the Holy Roman Empire. Frederick III made him poet laureate. He took holy orders in 1447 at the ripe age of forty-two, at which point he was made bishop of Trieste. He was transferred to the bishopric of Siena in 1450, made a cardinal in 1456, and elected pope as Pius II in 1458. An impressive feat given his childhood and his past life as a bawdy novelist.

For Piccolomini, education was certainly his salvation, and he believed that it was essential for being a successful man of the world and man of the Church. In 1450, he wrote an educational treatise for the teenaged King Ladislas of Hungary, who resided, like Piccolomini, at the imperial court at Vienna. It is a classic example of a Renaissance educational treatise, dedicated to a young person of elite status for whom humanist instruction was *de rigueur*. *On the Education of Boys* is a particularly valuable contribution to this subject as it is written by an Italian humanist for a non-Italian context. Other Renaissance theorists such as Vergerio and Guarino were writing for Italian princelings, who were entirely surrounded by the politics and culture of the Italian Renaissance. Ladislas was not among them. He had to prepare to be a defender of Christianity against the inroads of the Ottoman Turks in both action and thought, so Piccolomini's advice changed to deal with the realities of Central European rulership. It is, therefore, more explicitly militaristic than other educational treatises of this period. Piccolomini also engaged with the criticism of Italian humanism levelled by some in the German cultural milieu, who saw such instruction as, at best, useless, or at worst, godless. *On the Education of Boys* was a treatise designed to bring humanistic educational practices, which had been shaped over a century on the Italian peninsula, over the Alps to a new, occasionally hostile, audience. Piccolomini, writing in the aftermath of the rediscovery of the complete version of Quintilian's *Education of an Orator* (which he quotes), sought to consciously integrate classical and medieval educational traditions.

Schooling in Medieval Literature

While I have concentrated on didactic, prescriptive literature (works that were intentionally written to give advice on how to educate children), depictions of medieval schoolrooms and their inhabitants appear in the poetry, romances, and fond memoirs of the Middle Ages. And these too may provide information on life for teachers and pupils alike. For example, Jean Froissart in his poem *Un Galant de douze ans — A Courtly Lover at Twelve* — recounts the treats and gifts he would give to win the favour of the little girls at school, such as pins or an apple or pear.[16] But this is not just a sweet memory in a nice little ditty: instead, it tells us that Froissart appears to have attended school with girls. This sort of mixed schooling conflicts with traditional interpretations of both the prescriptive literature and the documentary evidence but may indeed have been the case in smaller schools and less-populated areas.

Among memoirs of the Middle Ages, those of Claude Bellièvre also give us a brief but surprisingly informative glimpse of his elementary education. As a future luminary of both municipal and royal administrations in sixteenth-century Lyon, he was educated in Toulouse and in Italy. His first lessons, however, were given to him on his family estate just outside Lyon by 'a good labourer called Ragot, who knew how to read'.[17] Again, this is a short remark in a much larger work but it tells us that even for a prominent bourgeois, professional family such as the Bellièvres, agricultural workers could act as teachers for their children. Ragot was not only literate but literate enough to teach — and may well have extended his services beyond the family of his employers to the children of other peasants and country people. The episode is a reminder that literacy was not only present in urban areas but was possessed — and likely desired — in the countryside too.[18]

Probably the most famous depiction of an elementary school in medieval imaginative literature is in Chaucer's 'The Prioress's Tale' from *The Canterbury Tales*. Known for its anti-Semitism and perpetuation of blood libel, the story revolves around a schoolboy who is killed by Jewish people in a city in Asia. Of interest to us is the description of the boy's experience at school where children were 'taught to sing and read' as 'was customary there'.[19] Our ill-fated hero was seven, learning from his 'primer', and still had no understanding of Latin. This suggests that he was still learning his alphabet and syllables and perhaps memorising prayers and thus agrees with much of what we know from contemporary records. Furthermore, he is distracted by other, older pupils learning to sing the hymn *Alma redemptoris*. He asks one of these older boys to translate the words and is given a vague summary of the content because...

> That's all that I can tell you of the matter,
> I'm learning singing, and don't know much grammar.[20]

This tells us that children at different levels were being taught in the same room and that an understanding of the Latin language was not necessarily the primary goal at this stage in elementary education. The one-room school was indeed a feature of the Middle Ages and beyond, as can be seen in woodcuts from the sixteenth century from the Low Countries and Germany — where dozens of pupils of differing ages and (sometimes) sexes are being instructed in different subjects in different parts of the same space.[21]

These three examples are a taste of the information available from literary representations of medieval schooling. Not only do these match the documentary sources available but they also overlap with the prescriptive literature. More research is needed in this area but a good start is Danièle Alexandre-Bidon and Marie-Thérèse Lorcin's book on medieval childhood and education which uses a cross-section of literary sources.[22]

***

As has been stated before, the selection presented here is not a comprehensive list of medieval literature on education. It has left out some important works, such as Alexander Neckham's *Sacerdos ad altare*, written in England around 1210, with its exhortations towards corporal punishment — 'without scourges and whips there is no means of correction' — and its extremely useful recommendations on textbooks.[23] There is no real discussion of the treatises written by important Italian pedagogues, Pier Paolo Vergerio's *The Character and Studies Befitting a Free-Born Youth* (1402–03) and Battista

Guarino's *A Programme of Teaching and Learning* (1459).[24] We have only scratched the surface of Jean Gerson's pedagogical writings, and have not even mentioned his *On Leading the Young to Christ* (*De parvulis ad Christum trahendis*) or his *Little Book of Proverbs for Schoolchildren* (*Livret-proverbes pour écoliers*). This side of Gerson's output deserves a great deal more attention than it has received in the past. This present little book, however, is intended to demonstrate the kind of information that is available in works like these. It is meant as a starting point for more in-depth studies of educational literature, both as sources for theoretical ideas and everyday instructional practice. The following sections will look at some of the common subjects that educational literature addressed throughout the Middle Ages.

II
The Beginning and End of Elementary and Grammar Education

THE MEDIEVAL DISCUSSION THAT EXAMINES WHEN children were supposed to begin formal schooling was dominated by the concept of the ages of man. While this idea was widely written about and commented upon, the main authority on this idea was Isidore of Seville (ca. 560–636). His definition of the ages of man, as laid out in his *Etymologies*, both reflected then current traditions and served as the pattern for later writers. Life was divided up into six stages of varying lengths: *infantia, pueritia, adolescentia, iuventus, aetas senioris,* and *senectus*. It is, of course, the first three of these 'ages' that we are interested in here. Each of these was seven years long; thus, *infantia* lasted from birth until the age of seven, *pueritia* lasted from seven until fourteen years of age, and *adolescentia* stretched from fourteen until the age of twenty-one.²⁵ It was during these stages, specifically the second one, that elementary and grammar instruction was supposed to take place. Most medieval commentators on education had fixed ideas on when this would begin, loosely based on the concept that certain activities were appropriate to certain ages. For example, when John of Salisbury described Bernard of Chartres's teaching of Latin composition, he used the word *puer* or boy when referring to Bernard's pupils. Authors do not appear to have been casual about the use of phrases relating to age.²⁶ While *infantia* might have represented the home and the control and care of the mother or other females of the household, *pueritia* represented, especially for boys, a period of preparation for adulthood, characterised by apprenticeship and school. This approach — that is, of a defined age for the beginning of education — is frequently discussed in educational treatises.

Not all the writers who discussed when a child should begin formal schooling agreed absolutely with the Isidorian partition between *infantia* and *pueritia*. Only one, the author of the *Commendation*, agreed that seven was the age to start. Quintilian, on the other hand, felt that seven was a good age to start school but should not be prescriptive, stating 'that no age should be without interest'.²⁷ Parents, nurses, and pedagogues (tutors) all had a role to play in the formation of a child's mind. Quintilian spends a certain amount of time discussing the importance of domestic influences on a nascent orator. Educated parents and well-spoken nurses contributed a great deal towards a child's development. Pedagogues (private tutors who were often employed in addition to sending the child to a master) and slaves should acknowledge their own short-comings in their knowledge and so on.[28] His focus was on ensuring that the time in life when memorisation came easily should not be wasted:

> Let us therefore not waste the earliest years, especially as the elements of reading and writing are entirely a matter of memory, which not only already exists in little children, but is at its most retentive.[29]

He does mention that seven was the generally agreed time to begin school but he himself believed that adherence to such a specific point was unnecessary. Both Philippe of Navarre and Giles of Rome concurred that formal education should start at a young, but undefined, age. Navarre calls on parents to set their sons to training for their intended vocations as soon as possible:

> You put the child to learn whatever occupation [...], and one must commence as early as one can.[30]

Giles of Rome concentrated on the importance of learning languages (that is, Latin) as early as possible, stating that those who did not learn it during their youth never achieved fluency.[31] This ambiguity of advice may have had two causes: the Isidorian scheme may have been so deeply entrenched that it was a given that children would begin formal schooling at seven or that the precise age of commencement was not seen as being standard across every child and every situation. The important thing was to get children started at school at a sufficiently young age to be able to exploit their youthful memory and to acclimatise them to the rigours of the classroom. Only three commentators recommended a precise age to begin school. The anonymous author of the *Commendation* was alone in his promotion of the supposed ideal of seven. In his exhortation to prospective clerics, he stated that those of 'seven summers' were 'ready for apprenticeship to letters'.[32] He proceeded to repeat this piece of advice twice:

> The true teacher of boys ought to consider carefully the different individualities of his pupils, for they come at seven, as the age of infancy is most often reckoned, to receive the first rudiments.[33]

He mentioned it again when discussing the elementary curriculum. For this anonymous author, writing so particularly about non-elite elementary and grammar education, beginning school at seven was fixed in both tradition and practice. Nowhere does he suggest that formal instruction of any kind should occur before this age. It is interesting to compare this with the recommendations of Philippe of Navarre who proposes that parents should teach their children their prayers and the articles of faith from as young an age as possible. It is likely that this is the actual experience of the boys attending the schools written about by the anonymous author but he himself is silent on this possibility. Vincent of Beauvais, in his

Speculum doctrinale, stated that boys should begin formal education at the age of six. He appeared to accept that this was relatively early; however, as he urged that the pupil should be taught slowly and methodically. Certainly, both the anonymous author of the *Commendation* and Vincent of Beauvais believed that a child beginning school should not be overburdened or strained. This reflects Quintilian's remark that too much pressure on the very young might very well have a detrimental effect on their academic progress:

> I am not so careless of age differences as to think that the very young should be forced on prematurely, and that set tasks should be demanded of them. For one of the first things to take care of is that the child, who is not yet able to love study, should not come to hate it and retain his fear of the bitter taste he has experienced even beyond his first years.[34]

Dubois, the last of our authors to stipulate an exact age to begin schooling, takes an opposite stance. His educational programme was influenced by relatively recent political and military events. Given that he wrote his treatise in the first decade of the fourteenth century, the fall of Acre in 1291 still cast a shadow. The pupils in his proposed schools were to be a new type of crusader and Dubois certainly felt that the sooner they began their training and education, the better. Boys and girls were to be selected at the age of four or five 'by a wise philosopher' who could ascertain their future potential.[35] As discussed in the section on the organisation of the school day, these selectees were immersed in an intensive educational curriculum, the goal of which was to create an army of colonists ready to be sent to the Holy Land as soon as possible. Dubois explained why he sought to speed up the educational process as follows:

> For the reasons cited it is well that youth progress so rapidly in the sciences that they come to practical experience in the full vigour and with the expectation of a long life in accordance with the presumption of law and nature.[36]

In comparison to the recommendations of other authors, this appears hasty. The desired outcome was not simply an educational or intellectual one but a geopolitical one that affected and, indeed, distorted the entire process. While the Isidorian ideal that seven was the border between *infantia* and *pueritia* is both convenient and attractive as a theory, there is little in other educational treatises to reinforce this as an absolute age when children began formal schooling.

Likewise, there is almost no discussion about when elementary or grammar education would end. In many ways, this was a more tenuous concept. Medieval commentators did not delineate the period during which someone was educated in a formal setting as a fixed length of time. There was no suggestion that elementary and grammar instruction would take seven full years, except in the work of the author of the *Commendation*. The central argument for this flexible and less-constrictive approach was this: pupils were deemed to have mastered a certain subject when they had, in fact, mastered it. Only then could they move on to the next text or the next subject or to a higher institution of learning. Most commentators did not see and did not have to see the instructional process as a race to meet any kind of target regarding age and a pre-specified level of academic achievement. This attitude may have its basis in the idea that not all children learned at the same rate. Developmental landmarks were personal things, particular to the individual child, and medieval pedagogical writers seem to have accepted this. This will be discussed in more detail later on, in the section on natural ability.

Some authors, however, did state when this stage of education should end in their opinion. Dubois, as a result of an early start and an accelerated curriculum, stated that children should have finished the entirety of the course in grammar at the age of twelve at the latest.[37] At this point, boys would be sent to the 'schools of logic' and be hearing formal lectures by fourteen.[38] The author of the *Commendation* recommended that fourteen was the proper time to finish the full grammar curriculum. By that age, the pupils would be ready for the more difficult subjects of logic and rhetoric:

> For then the light of reason begins to gleam
> in him and then is the time to propound the
> involutions of dialectic to the brighter and

better pupils together with the examples of fine rhetoric.[39]

It is clear that fixed-term courses in elementary and grammar studies were not envisioned by medieval theorists. Apart from the anonymous author of the *Commendation* and Pierre Dubois, authors were vague about when such instruction should begin and end. In fact, they viewed this concept as being inherently variable. They appear to have been aware of the numerous factors that might advance or delay the beginning of formal education such as financial success or pressure, physical proximity to a school or the character of the children themselves. Indeed, even amongst the authors discussed in this work, we have an example of a would-be student whose educational career did not smoothly progress from grammar instruction to university at any kind of fixed age. While most young men started at the *studio* in Siena at the age of fourteen, Aeneas Silvius Piccolomini, noted humanist and future pope, started at the age of eighteen. His entry had been delayed due to his family's financial difficulties and it had only been through the offer of free board and lodgings from a relative that he ever made it there at all.

III
Organising the School Day and Schoolroom

TIMETABLING AND CLASSROOM SET-UP WERE DAILY practicalities of teaching and learning that attracted the opinions of pedagogical commentators in the Middle Ages. Several writers outlined their own concept of what should happen in the schoolroom and when it should happen. Some went so far as to describe how the classroom itself should appear. From these suggestions, we can construct what the school day might have looked like and how theorists felt that their suggestions affected learning in a positive way.

There is surprisingly little information about precisely what time in the day teaching was supposed to start. Even Quintilian and Gerson, usually so loquacious, are silent on the timing. What information there is, however, points to a fairly standard pattern for the school day that had begun to emerge by the later Middle Ages. Teaching took place throughout the daylight hours.[40] Class length and subject changed depending on the season. Evening sessions were common when the stretch in the summer evenings allowed. There were specific times for learning new material, revision, examination, and review of behaviour. The medieval school day was supposed to be well organised, with compartmentalised activities and daily goals. In schools attached to religious houses and churches, *terce* or another morning service might have signalled the start of school.[41] It is, of course, likely that classes began relatively early in the morning and made the most of the daylight hours. According to commentators, the school day was relatively full, especially for those who were boarding at school.

Pierre Dubois, in his *Recovery of the Holy Land*, lays out a particularly intense day for the children undergoing his unique vision of education.[42] Once they had finished the introductory course consisting of the alphabet and syllables, the pupils studying the elementary grammar course had to cover the Psalter, singing, and Donatus during the day. The singing lesson was to take place during 'the third part of the day' and Donatus was to be studied 'at other hours'. It is difficult to understand what Dubois meant by the third part of the day. It could mean *terce* or nine o'clock in the morning or it could signify the afternoon (if the day is divided into four parts: morning, lunchtime, afternoon, evening). This can be compared to Gerson's plan for the choirboys of Paris. He stated that grammar should be studied by the boys from morning to lunch (probably 9am to 12pm) and 'from the return from vespers up to dinner'.[43] This later class undoubtedly changed its time and possibly even its length depending on the time of year but would have occurred sometime between 4pm and 7pm. If Dubois's 'third part of the day' is understood as 9am, then this differs from Gerson, who assigned that period to grammatical studies and who suggests that this allocation of the morning to grammar was the 'hour more usual for such things'.[44] According to Gerson, singing, a subject of paramount importance for choirboys, should be taught at unspecified 'set hours' and in a way that did not impinge on the grammar curriculum.[45] While Gerson's day does not appear to change depending on the age and academic advancement of the choirboys, Dubois's day changes radically when his budding crusaders begin reading the elementary Latin works and studying more advanced grammatical texts. The day also differed depending on the time of year. During the summer, Cato and other minor authors were introduced in 'four long lessons a day, or as much as his natural capacity can stand; let [the pupil] not go to sleep over these.'[46] This would strongly suggest that this was an intense reading course and that it would not be out of the ordinary for pupils to become exhausted or bored. During the winter, grammar (probably Alexander of Villedieu's *Doctrinale* and the *Graecisimus*) was studied.[47] The evenings were given over to Latin composition.

While Dubois's pedagogical blueprint was radical and extremely challenging for prospective pupils, there was a reason for this and it does appear to mimic other descriptions and prescriptions of the medieval school day. Dubois's idea was to speed up the entire course of studies so that children could move on quickly to further training and not spend their healthiest, most robust years in the classroom when they could be recovering the Holy Land:

> It is well that youth progress so rapidly in the sciences that they come to practical experience in full vigour and with the expectation of a long life in accordance with the presumption of law and nature.[48]

Yet, despite the unique and bellicose ambition behind Dubois's recommendation, intense courses of study were part of the wider pedagogical culture of the later Middle Ages. Several aspects of Bernard of Chartres's classroom practice (as described by John of Salisbury) were similar to those advocated by Dubois. Bernard's evening revision course in grammar was also relatively intensive:

> if anyone were to take part in it for an entire year, provided he were not a dullard, he would become thoroughly familiar with the correct method of speaking and writing.[49]

Bernard's students may have required this acceleration owing to financial pressures or, more likely, to limited time available, since many were attached to other religious institutions that would have required their presence. As in Dubois's advice, Bernard also had his students practise their Latin composition on a daily basis:

> A further feature of Bernard's method was to have his disciples compose prose and poetry

every day, and exercise their faculties in mutual conferences [...][50]

It is likely that these exercises took place at the same time (that is, in the evening) as Bernard's 'declination' or 'philosophical collation'. This was when Bernard took his students through their grammatical paces as described above. For Dubois, the evening was also given over to Latin composition; indeed, this activity was completely restricted to the evenings.[51] The evening in Gerson's scheme was when boys who misbehaved during the day were punished by the master:

> And these failures will be able to be recorded [...], and at the end of the day presented to the master, so that he may frequently correct failings.[52]

The end of the day, in other words, was reserved for review of both what the pupils had learned and their conduct. Even the composition exercises recommended by Dubois were a form of revision and the more advanced grammar instruction given by Bernard was presented as reflection and discussion on the topics covered during the day.[53] Only Ælfric Bata suggested that the revision exercises may have taken place in the morning:

> Read and memorise your assignments so that first thing tomorrow morning you can recite quickly and then learn more from our teacher.[54]

It is unclear if Dubois, John of Salisbury, and Gerson felt that the evening review was part of the school day proper or if it was something extra. It is also unclear if these writers considered the practicalities of teaching (and especially the physical task of reading and writing) after dark. It is likely that nightfall brought the school day to a close and that only in the most lavishly-funded schools, such as those funded by the wealth of the Templars in Dubois's fantasy, could lessons have been expected to continue.[55]

We only gleam information about a pupil's day from monastic sources, specifically from Ælfric Bata's scenes set in a late Anglo-Saxon monastery. In Colloquy 5, a master questions his pupils about how they have spent their day. The boys of course report that they have been hard at work and on their best behaviour.

- Before *prime* (6am) — writing
- Between *prime* and *terce* (6am–9am) — writing
- Toilet
- Sang the seven penitential psalms (clearly in their own classroom)
- Sang prayers in church
- Participated in Mass
- Mealtime in the refectory
- Toilet again (this time singing their 'verse')
- Back at school and ready to learn[56]

It is unclear exactly how much of the day these boys were relating to their teacher. Nicholas Orme suggests that this is their entire day but perhaps it simply covers their morning, with classes proper only beginning after *terce* followed by a full Mass (after 10am). That unfortunately does not explain the mealtime but perhaps it was a mid-morning snack after an admittedly active morning for the boys.[57]

The school day, however, was not one long grind of lessons and constant reviews stretching into the evening. Pedagogical commentators were not so harsh as to deny school children rest and holiday. Vincent of Beauvais, though very strict in other areas, accepted that children should not be sent to school every day and most other writers (with the notable exception of Pierre Dubois) felt that some sort of daily recess and play was essential for the effective instruction of the young.[58] Quintilian is eloquent on this subject:

> Everyone must be given some relaxation, not only because there is nothing that can stand perpetual strain — even things which are without sense or life need to be relaxed by periods of rest in order to preserve their strength — but also because study depends on the will to learn, and this cannot be forced.[59]

This example is followed by both Jean Gerson and the anonymous author of the *Commendation of the Clerk*. The latter sees the usefulness of active play in reviving the flagging spirits of the hard-working schoolboy:

> Nor should the scholars be always kept intent upon their books and writing tablets, but they should be given an occasional recess and set at suitable games, so that their spirits may be raised and their blood stirred by the pleasure of play. For thus the boys' minds which before were fatigued by the tedium of classes are refined and refreshed.[60]

While Gerson agrees with the necessity of games and play, he is more concerned with the nature of the games that boys should be allowed to indulge in:

> Furthermore, let all games be forbidden to them that derive from greed or sexual impropriety or degrading shouting, or from anger, and rancour, as is the game of dice or risk and all similar things, let whatever be exercised in moderation [...] play with the hoop, shun the dice.[61]

In this, Gerson reflects the pronouncements of both Quintilian and the author of the *Commendation*. Quintilian recommends that learning be combined into play:

> There are even some games which are useful for sharpening the wits, for example competitions in which they ask one another all sorts of little questions.[62]

Suitable games were allowed but anything that encouraged gambling or exultation in violence was to be avoided. This is of particular interest when one considers the frequency of school-sanctioned cock-fights in the Middle Ages. In William FitzStephen's description of London in the twelfth century, boys from various schools — with the blessing and participation of their teachers — would bring their fighting birds to a prearranged place on Shrove Tuesday and devote the morning to watching.[63] The subject of play within the context of a school is certainly one of those moments where the fine ideas of theorists were not always followed on the ground.

Gerson also gives an opinion about when playtime and periods of relaxation should take place. He suggests that after lunch and dinner 'when [the boys] are less able for other serious things'.[64] The other authors are silent on when recreation should take place. Perhaps it was dependant on how the class was progressing, the difficulty of the subject being taught, and how the pupils were responding. Given the general flexibility of the medieval school day with regards to when it began and ended, the teachers could decide themselves on the timing of recess.[65] This precise situation appears in the *Colloquies* of Ælfric Bata when the master allows the boys to play outside with their sticks, hoops, and balls (just as Gerson suggested) because they had time before vespers and had already memorised their set assignments.[66] Other breaks were provided for lunch and dinner and, in schools where pupils were also boarders, naps were also timetabled. It is likely that children who attended schools adjacent to their homes would have returned there in order to eat, thus providing some exercise and respite from the lessons. Nevertheless, recess was expected to be built into the medieval school day.

***

The organisation of the physical schoolroom, however, was not so widely discussed in pedagogical literature. There was no such thing as the perfect space in which to hold a class. Most writers do not even consider this notion and the archival evidence backs this up.[67] School was held wherever was convenient. A room and some benches were all that was required. In the context of religious institutions, the schoolroom could be anywhere. Even a shady tree in more sunny climates was acceptable. There were, occasionally, tangible provisions made for teaching spaces. At Saint-Paul in Lyon, school appears to have been held in a room above the chapel of Sainte-Catherine. At the cathedral of Saint-Jean in Lyon, a designated classroom and dormitory was only created in the 1390s and at Notre Dame in Paris in the 1450s. Only one commentator takes the time to describe what the perfect classroom was, in his opinion. The anonymous author of the *Commendation of the Clerk* goes into some detail about the construction and layout of the schoolroom.[68] Firstly, there must be two classrooms, if possible, a summer one and a winter one. The summer one should be well-ventilated and face north while the winter one should be tightly enclosed so that it can be more effectively heated 'with burning coals according to the custom of the region'. The author states that some masters actually build their schools into the slope of a hill and panel them with planks of fir or pine. Given that the anonymous author of the *Commendation of the Clerk* was likely from Germanic lands (possibly Austria), his advice here is clearly tailored for teachers who might be in a position to oversee the building of a dedicated schoolhouse in a rural or semi-rural area where land and materials were freely available and where said schoolhouse could be easily built into the side of a hill. His discussion here also raises some questions about his intended audience. Did he write for teachers who were venturing into Central Europe in much the same way as later educators would into the American West? That question cannot be answered but it is clear that such principles of design would not have been on the minds of most medieval teachers.

In the often crowded towns and cities of the Middle Ages, space was at a premium.[69] It appears that, in reality, most schooling took place in one room where all the pupils, regardless of age or level of advancement, were seated on benches, and that sometimes class took place in the house or the very room where the teacher lived. Guilbert of Nogaret's first teacher (beyond his mother) taught a small group of boys in his own chamber. As for the decoration of the school, information such as alphabets and prayers may have been inscribed onto wall charts or directly onto the walls themselves.[70] The focus of the classroom, however, was the teacher, and it is most likely that pupils gathered around his or her chair. The physical organisation of the classroom mattered less than the organisation of the school day to medieval commentators. The school was not a physical place in the medieval mind but rather the collective of people made up of teachers and pupils: wherever they gathered was the school.

IV
Corporal Punishment

THE SUBJECT OF CORPORAL PUNISHMENT WAS A controversial one amongst those who commented on medieval education. This is surprising considering the iconography of the teacher in images from the Middle Ages and Renaissance. The grammar master was almost always depicted with a switch or a bundle of twigs, forever poised to deal out lashes for mistakes and bad behaviour. The image of the teacher was also the image of a disciplinarian. Some of the pedagogical literature reinforces this view of medieval education while other authors opposed the use of violence in the classroom. Some theorists sought a middle way, struggling between the necessity for punishment and the fear that such action might destroy a child's will to learn. Such differences in opinions produced vigorous debate. Writers quote everything from long dead Roman teachers to the Bible to support their own arguments. They often explicitly objected to each other's positions on the subject. The question of corporal punishment, to spare the rod or not, demonstrates a theoretical dispute that reflects something of the real medieval classroom, where a narrow line had to be walked by masters, between abuse and too much leniency. Both extremes could lead to the loss of reputation and paying pupils.

Several authors advocated the use of corporal punishment by medieval teachers but few did so without suggesting some sort of limitation or moderation. There is a sense of caution even in the most enthusiastic endorsements for the practice. Only the rule of Saint Benedict is unequivocal in promoting corporal punishment, specifically for children. Adult members of the monastery were only punished (in an undefined manner) if they refused to admit that they had made a mistake in choir. Children, on the other hand, were subject to immediate physical correction:

> If anyone shall have made a mistake in psalm, responsory, or antiphon or lection and unless he shall have there and then humbly made satisfaction before all, let him be subjected to severe punishment as one who was unwilling to correct by humility what by negligence he had done amiss. But in the case of children, let them, for the like fault, be whipped.[71]

Augustine was the most enigmatic when it came to the question of beating in an educational context. At first glance, he appears to actively approve of corporal punishment, linking it with earthly suffering and punishment for sinfulness:

> I did not love learning and hated being forced to learn. Since I was forced, good was done to me, although I myself did not do well. I would not learn unless I was compelled. But nobody does well against his will even if what he does is good [...] But you, Lord [...] used the mistakes of those who urged me to study for my advantage. But my own error, consisting of my unwillingness to learn, you used for my punishment. This was a punishment well deserved by one who was so small a boy but so great a sinner.[72]

Further on in the *Confessions*, Augustine even appears to suggest that corporal punishment has a redemptory purpose:

> Nevertheless, by the dictates of your laws, O God, compulsion acts to restrain the free flow of curiosity. These laws are imposed by torments which range from the canes of teachers to the sufferings of the martyrs and have the effect of mingling in us a life-giving bitterness, which summons us back to You from the soul-destroying pleasure which first influenced us to turn our backs on You.[73]

The rod of the master was changed, therefore, into a conduit for salvation, a righteous judgement on the misdeeds of little children.[74] For Augustine, such judgement was necessary for the ultimate salvation of the souls of those who received it but he was less enamoured of the practice when it came to helping pupils make real advances in their studies. Augustine's personal struggles with the Greek language will be discussed again but we must consider them here in the context of the academic efficacy of corporal punishment:

> I knew none of the Greek words and I was unrelentingly driven to learn by savage threats and punishments. But at one period of my life, when I was a young child, I knew no Latin. Yet I learned it without fear or torture, merely by noticing what went on around me amid the flattering words of nurses, the jokes of people who smiled on me, and the joyful humours of people who played with me. I learned my own language, without the pressure of those who compelled me with punishment.[75]

The suggestion here was that physical chastisement did not always function as an effective learning tool. This ambiguity in Augustine set the tone for the medieval discussion on punishment in the classroom. What was good for the soul might not be good for learning and might indeed erode away the will to learn in children.

Vincent of Beauvais carried on this uncertainty in his work on education. At the beginning of his *On the Education of Noble Children*, he wrote a lengthy meditation on Ecclesiasticus 7:25, 'Hast thou children? Instruct them, and bow down their neck from childhood'. Vincent made full use of the Bible and the Church Fathers in his consideration of corporal punishment. He quoted biblical commentary on Jeremiah 6:8, 'Through every pain and scourge you will learn, Jerusalem'.[76] He quoted Cyprian, 'Teaching is the well-ordered reproof of habits.'[77] His conclusion, which he returned to several times in his first chapter alone, was that physical punishment was good for children:

> Not only must the boys be instructed with words, but also, if it is beneficial, with whips.[78]

The theological reason for the importance of corporal punishment followed directly on from Augustine. Childhood, by its very nature, was evil and children were prone to evil and had to be bent or bowed down from their youth in order to train their souls:

> Therefore, since childhood is wild and insolent towards learning and hesitant about being well conducted, truly prone to evil, it is therefore right that, after it was said, 'teach these', it is added, 'and bend them, from their childhood.'[79]

Nevertheless, Vincent of Beauvais suggested that too much bending may break the subject. He quoted from Book 1 of Quintilian's *The Education of an Orator*, 'For you may break easily what you would correct'.[80] This served as a warning to those who used undue and immoderate discipline in the classroom. While Vincent felt it was necessary for the moral health of the child, just as Augustine had, it could go too far and could be counterproductive in the classroom. Indeed, he even dedicated one of the chapters in *On the Education of Noble Children* to the subject of moderate coercion (Chapter XXVI, *De cohercionis moderacione*) — 'regarding teaching, three aspects of punishment are required, namely severity, clemency and discretion or moderation'.[81] In order to curb the worst excesses of corporal punishment, Vincent advocated that punishment be mingled with leniency and, when punishment was unavoidable, he laid out guidelines on how best to carry it out. He divides these into method, timing, and place.[82] Correct method required good intention, genuine purpose, and restraint.[83] Timing had to be thought out to prevent unpremeditated punishment which could lead to the use of excessive force and the loss of control on the part of the teacher:

> Timing should be heeded as well, as censuring the offending party should not be employed immediately as if during a rage, but always be put off to a later suitable time. For it is read in *Proverbs* 29: 'All his spirit', that is anger, 'advances foolishness, wisdom truly delays and reserves for the future.' So

> again not all faults should be punished, but
> they should be given way to for a later time.[84]

Rage and recklessness with the rod was recognised as a dangerous consequence of corporal punishment. Vincent was aware that injury and intemperance were possibilities but he advised that the teacher leave punishment until a later time, rather than refrain from chastisement completely. A later time would allow tempers to cool and discipline appropriate to the misdemeanour to be handed down.

Gerson recommended a similar approach. There were many reasons why choirboys might need to be reprimanded and Gerson provides a fairly comprehensive list: speaking French, swearing, lying, deceiving others, speaking badly, striking another, speaking shamefully or unchastely, rising from bed late, failing to observe the Hours or chattering in church. All these things resulted in a note being made beside the name of the boy on a list. This list was handed to the master of the school who would 'correct failings' at the end of each day.[85] Immediate punishment was only received if a boy struck one of his fellows. Wrongdoing was dealt with, therefore, in a calm and controlled fashion. Indeed, in Gerson's scheme, the masters of grammar and song who were, presumably, the ones who recorded the errors of their charges, did not carry out the sentence. This was given over to their superior, the master of the school. Ideally, this meant that any residual anger or embarrassment was removed from the equation. It also lent a psychological feature to the disciplinary process. Any pupil who had broken the rules had to wait until evening to receive their punishment. It is easy to imagine the feelings of foreboding that this method must have caused. Place was equally important as time and method. While Gerson's punishments did not appear to have taken place in front of the whole host of boys, Vincent of Beauvais suggested that the public or private nature of the punishment should match the error:

> Finally place must also be observed, mainly because if the sin should be hidden, the punishment must be secret [...] However, if it should be flagrant, correction should be done in the open.[86]

Gerson and Vincent differ considerably from what is depicted in Ælfric Bata's *Colloquies*. In Colloquy 28, the master punishes a boy who has stolen apples from the monastery, in fact a repeat offender. Not only is the boy beaten in front of his classmates, but two are enlisted to actually carry out the punishment.[87] Even Vincent, who embraced the validity of corporal punishment, felt that limits had to be imposed. Because there was an idea that punishment could be done in different ways or could have different purposes, the debate in medieval pedagogical literature thus acquired substantial nuance. Those who advocated physical chastisement tended not to do so without some discussion of the reasons for it or without the imposition of limits and restraints.

Some authors, however, rejected corporal punishment completely. These include such luminaries as Quintilian and Jerome. It is of great interest to examine why a classical or medieval teacher would object to the practice. Firstly, there was the idea that too much abuse and criticism would cripple a child academically. Fear was seen as a fickle aid in the teaching process. Piccolomini, for example, states that boys 'visited with much criticism [...] become broken and low-spirited'.[88] He was, however, referring to Quintilian when he wrote this. The old orator was very particular in his opposition to physical punishment. When correction was too severe it served to disable all the better faculties of a child:

> We should not even admonish that which is unworthy, the yokes of boys are many [and] at the same time to fail because of the severity of correction, they both despair and grieve and, in the end, they hate and that hurts the most, as long as they are afraid of everything, they attempt nothing.[89]

The central purpose of the learning process, the acquisition of knowledge, was often shown to be threatened by the use of force. If children could not learn effectively in such circumstances, then the practice of physical chastisement had to be set aside.

Secondly, corporal punishment affected the character and attitude of the pupil. Beatings were not a useful pedagogical tool if they were employed on a daily basis for academic mistakes in the classroom. Quintilian and Piccolomini both felt that it would make certain students intractable and harden them towards the act of learning. Piccolomini states:

> Indeed, from blows arises a hatred which endures even to manhood, yet nothing is worse for a pupil than to hate his teachers.[90]

He was clearly referencing Quintilian in this sentiment:

> if a boy is so lacking in self-respect that reproof is powerless to put him right, he will even become hardened to blows, like the worst type of slave.[91]

Even if the teacher felt that corporal punishment was necessary, it had the potential to elicit quite the opposite reaction from the child. Pupils might start to refuse consciously or subconsciously to learn or to obey as a form of resistance against discipline. Grudges could be formed and such feelings could affect the adult lives of the children in question. Quintilian has a particularly nuanced perception of the long-term consequences:

> Though you may compel a child with blows, what can you do with a young man who cannot be threatened like this and who has more important lessons to learn?[92]

The implications of corporal punishment were, therefore, widespread and prolonged. The emotional aftermath was identified as a serious drawback by pedagogical writers and Quintilian and Piccolomini clearly believed that the possibility of accidentally encouraging bad traits in their pupils was enough to refrain from the practice of physical punishment altogether.

Thirdly, some theorists felt that there were other, better incentives to learning. Encouragement and a little healthy competition could get better results than fear and abuse. Positive reinforcement was the basis of Jerome's approach to discipline:

> You must not scold her if she is somewhat slow; praise is the best sharpener of wits.[93]

Quintilian also advocates constant and conscientious supervision. Punishment was rarely necessary when someone had made sure that the child did what they were supposed to do.[94] Competition too could prompt children to learn without any kind of reprimand, physical or verbal. For Quintilian, word games had the potential to help pupils without competing in the context of the classroom. Jerome strongly supported the presence of companions for Paula, the subject of one of his pedagogical letters. Despite the fact that Paula was to be brought up in a sheltered way in order to prepare her as a handmaid of the Lord, classmates were seen as an important and non-violent way to encourage her:

> Let her have companions too in her lessons, so that she may seek to rival them and be stimulated by any praise they win [...] Let her be glad when she is first and sorry when she falls behind.[95]

By providing the young girl with peers, Jerome sought to stimulate the natural tendency towards competition and rivalry in children and channel the energy it created into learning. It should also be noted that Jerome was not in the least upset by the use of 'bribes' in encouraging young children to learn. In both his letter to Laeta and his letter to Pacatula, liberal rewards of things that might interest the very young were to be given. For example:

> To get her to repeat her lessons in her little shrill voice she must have a prize of a honey cake offered to her.[96]

Discussion of why physical punishment should *not* be implemented shows us ancient and medieval writers approached the issue with a considerable amount of nuance and sensitivity. There is a high level of understanding of how beatings could affect the academic progress of a pupil as well as their emotional well-being. Other mechanisms like rewards and the creation of a competitive environment were actively promoted as effective pedagogical tools.

There were many authors who promoted a mixed approach to corporal punishment in the classroom. This is linked to the concept of natural ability and the personal traits of individual pupils. While not all children learned at the same rate, not all children reacted in the same way to a beating or to a verbal scolding. It is here that the fear of impairing the academic progress of an individual child comes into play. Quintilian was the first to voice this fear and his dictum — 'as long as they are afraid of everything, they attempt nothing' — made its way into the work of Vincent of Beauvais, amongst others.[97] Not all pupils could be punished and not all crimes merited physical retribution. The anonymous author of the *Commendation of the Clerk* was one such theorist who felt that chastisement should be tailored to the recipient. For each character type, a different technique had to be used. For the 'frivolous', those who fought against learning and the authority of the master, the rod was necessary. For those who were shy, words would be sufficient.[98] Likewise, John of Salisbury recorded that Bernard of Chartres chose between exhortation and flogging in order to encourage his students to absorb their lessons.[99] There was a clear understanding by medieval teachers that not everything could be achieved by force and intimidation. The personality of the child had to be considered as well as, in the case of Bernard, the nature of the crime:

> And if, to embellish his work, someone had sewed on a patch of cloth filched from an external source, Bernard, on discovering this, would rebuke him for his plagiarism, but would generally refrain from punishing him. After he had reproved the student [...], he would, with modest indulgence, bid the boy to rise to real imitation of the [classical authors].[100]

It is clear that misbehaviour and delinquency in the classroom were not tolerated and were swiftly dealt with by means of corporal punishment. John of Salisbury's story, however, suggests that, at least sometimes, such punishments were not given out for shortcomings in their school work. Even the cardinal sin of laziness leading to plagiarism — when a pupil copied another's work — was not countered with the rod. This approach was opposed by Gerson's insistence that 'mistakes' such as speaking French would result in some sort of reprimand, though it is unclear if such a crime was met with words or a rod.[101] It is probable that this mixed approach, adjusting punishment in terms of the would-be recipient and the error, was the standard in the medieval classroom.

Punishment and, specifically, corporal punishment was a subject that provoked a certain intensity of debate among medieval pedagogical authors. The intricacy of the discussion and the variety of positions that were taken across the spectrum of opinion, points to a deep awareness of what a beating or a flogging might represent to a child. Proponents and opponents and even those who presented an ambiguous view of corporal punishment all sought to construct a rational basis for the adherence (or not) to the practice. Even those who advocated the exercise of physical chastisement laid out limits and fail-safes and accepted that excess was dangerous, both to the pupil and to the reputation of the teacher.

V
Natural Ability

ALMOST ALL MEDIEVAL THEORISTS ON EDUCATION accepted that natural ability was a factor in learning and teaching. It was recognised that not all children learned in the same way or at the same speed, that levels of aptitude varied, and that degrees of interest and engagement differed radically. Given that the intended audience of this literature was principally made up of those who taught rather than pupils themselves, there was an attempt by some authors to point out the reality of teaching a mixed-ability group. Some even went so far as to outline the drawbacks of using the same approach with each pupil. Though this may seem obvious to anyone who had ever been a teacher, the fact that the subject of pupil capacity was discussed in such length and that recommendations were given to help the school master indicate that medieval theorists accepted that children had characteristics and abilities that did not allow for absolutely standardised methods.

The first thing that authors tend to discuss when considering the abilities of pupils was their nature and characteristics when the children began school. The physical traits of the children had to be examined and their actions and personal manners had to be observed by the teacher. This was supposed to help the teacher predict a given child's capacity for learning. Dubois had a roving 'wise philosopher', who was tasked with selecting children of both genders. He had to 'recognise their probable natural aptitude for making progress in philosophical studies'.[102] Their entrance to school therefore depended on one individual, the 'wise philosopher'. Dubois stated that those selected would have 'heads well shaped and apt for making progress'.[103] Physical characteristics were, therefore, very important in the medieval mind for judging future success in the classroom. The Pseudo-Boethian *On the Teaching of School*, for example, bluntly rejected any physical ailment in prospective pupils:

> The deformed should not be a scholar.[104]

The anonymous author of the *Commendation* also encouraged teachers to consider four things: 'the state of the weather, a normal body, the physical constitution, and the mental capacity'.[105] All three of these writers felt that bodily health was important. While Dubois needed physically strong pupils ready for the duties and deprivations of crusading, the author of the *Commendation* suggested that the healthier the boy, the better their endurance within the classroom itself. Learning was not a physical challenge but good health was still seen as a desirable attribute. Intellectual and academic talent was the other characteristic that teachers had to ascertain in their newest pupils. For Quintilian, the best features to find in a young child were a good memory and the ability to imitate:

> As soon as a boy is entrusted to him, the skilled teacher will first spy out his ability and his nature. In children, the principal sign of talent is memory. There are two virtues of memory: quickness of grasp, and accurate retention. Next comes imitation; this also is a mark of a teachable nature, provided that it is exercised on what he is learning, not on someone's bearing or walk or some observable defect.[106]

These formed the foundation of effective learning. Ælfric Bata's master was also fully aware of his pupils' abilities. On hearing one boy excusing the others' lack of progress in memorising and reciting their work by saying 'they don't have good enough heads to recite every day', the teacher replied:

> Indeed, I know very well what kind of brains they have. You shouldn't say that to me. But this is your excuse, since you always excuse them.[107]

It was the business of the teacher to know exactly what kind of children they were dealing with. And that evaluation was quickly made by a prospective teacher, as the author of the *Commendation* indicates:

> The mental capacity of boys in the process of learning is quickly ascertained. For in the same kind of composition, some are found bright, others brighter, and others brightest of all. So also some are dull, others duller, and others so dull that their mind is despaired of.[108]

What we find here are two assertions that seem to contradict each other. Firstly, that a child must be of good bodily health to be a good pupil and secondly, that mental ability is the only factor that actually determines a child's future academic success. These are not as inconsistent as they may initially appear. The anonymous author of the *Commendation*, for example, is thinking in purely practical terms. If a child, no matter how bright and brilliant, cannot come to school because they are frequently ill, they may not be able to benefit fully from the instruction on offer. A child possessing of less natural talent but a strong constitution, however, could at the very least be eventually compelled to learn the fundamentals of Latin literacy. Of course, such recommendations do not cast a favourable light on the contemporary prejudices towards disability.

Following on from determining children's abilities, teachers were advised about how best to encourage their pupils and to make the best of their nascent talents. Each type of child was to be led towards knowledge along a different route. Gentle admonition might suffice for some but beatings might be the only way to turn a child towards the discipline and steadiness required to learn. Others might not respond to criticism at all and need positive reinforcement. The anonymous author of the *Commendation* gave the strongest guidance to masters on this matter:

> Therefore let the teacher of boys so direct them that he corrects the timid by words, masters the frivolous with rods, and bestows upon each according to his exigencies the gift of letters.[109]

Quintilian also accepted that differing teaching methods were necessary:

> The teacher must next consider how the pupil's mind should be handled. Some are idle unless you press them; other are impatient of discipline. Fear restrains some and paralyses others. Some need continuous effort to knock them into shape; with others, the sudden attack is more effective.[110]

This is reflected again in John of Salisbury's *Metalogicon*. Bernard of Chartres was wont to adjust his teaching style and the level of difficulty of the subject depending on his audience:

> He would do so [that is, teach], however, without trying to teach everything at one time. On the contrary, he would dispense his instruction to his hearers gradually, in a manner commensurate with their powers of assimilation.[111]

John of Salisbury also found that exhortations towards perfection only worked on some, while flogging was indispensable in the case of others.[112] The discussion of how to interact and direct individual pupils demonstrates that medieval thinkers accepted that children were different and that teachers had to treat them differently in order to instruct them effectively. This may seem obvious, especially for anyone who has ever taught, but it underlines the interest theoretical authors had in real classroom practice. Children were not empty vessels presented to a master. At no point do any of the writers who discussed natural ability and teaching method suggest that individually-tailored instruction was only for the elite or for the smaller classroom. While of course this kind of approach would have been increasingly constrained with each additional pupil, the need to consider natural aptitude was seen as a necessary part of successful teaching.

Another facet of the pedagogical literature on the subject of natural ability was the acceptance that not all students would thrive and flourish in the Latin curricula of the late Middle Ages. Certain authors did not see failure in a course of studies in Latin grammar as complete academic failure. There was always something else that an unsuccessful pupil could do. Perhaps this somewhat-lessened condemnatory tone was influenced by Augustine, who, in his *Confessions*, admitted to his own struggles with Greek language studies:

> The hard labour of completely mastering a foreign language mingled all the charming quality of the Greek tales with poison. For I knew none of the Greek words and I was unrelentingly driven to learn by savage threats and punishments.[113]

Even if the child was willing and even if the master was a good and attentive one (though this was not the case in Augustine's experience, according to his own recollections), the outcome was not necessarily secure. In the *Recovery of the Holy Land*, Dubois accepted that not all his would-be crusaders would be expert theologians or preachers or even literate in Latin. Dubois constructed a sliding scale of 'failure' depending on when children or youths were found to have gone as far as their natural capabilities could take them. At the top of this scale were those who had completed both the courses in grammar and logic and had progressed to the study of natural sciences and biblical exegesis. They had fallen at the next hurdle, however: the study of preaching, law, or medicine, and were to be directed to human or veterinary surgery.[114] Next were those who had been unable to grasp foreign languages such as Greek, Arabic, and Chaldean.[115] These pupils were taught how to read and write in their native French language. Dubois does not make it clear if they had failed in the study of these 'oriental' languages alone or whether Latin is included. It is likely that he would not have considered Latin as a foreign language and so these were the children who mastered only Latin and French. This was hardly a mean accomplishment but it was certainly seen as a handicap for those intended to spend most of their lives in the Middle East. Finally were the children who, despite the judgement of the 'wise philosopher', were unable even to master elementary Latin grammar.[116] These were to be trained in blacksmithing and carpentry but also in the construction of instruments of war (such as Roger Bacon's burning mirrors). In Dubois's scheme, something was always found to suit the talents of individual pupils as his crusade was to be a comprehensive one made up of all the most useful parts of French society. How could a colony succeed without those who could build and fix and work with their hands? Hugh of Saint-Victor was probably the most eloquent defender of those who were less able academically. Unlike Dubois, he did not quickly redirect them to other studies and pursuits but instead chose to hold them up as a model of consistency and hard work:

> There are many persons whose nature has left them so poor in ability that they can hardly grasp with their intellect even easy things [...] There are those who, while they are not unaware of their own dullness, nonetheless struggle after knowledge with all the effort they can put forth and who, by tirelessly keeping up their pursuit, deserve

to obtain as a result of their willpower what they by no means possess as a result of their work.[117]

Indeed, Hugh of Saint-Victor's deliberations on the concept of natural ability are the most subtle of all the authors examined in this section. While the anonymous author of the *Commendation* touched on the idea that almost all pupils, with effective teaching, should at least finish his course in grammar, Hugh of Saint-Victor demonstrated that talent was not enough.[118] For him, truly weak students were those who knew 'that they are in no way able to compass the highest things, [and so] neglect even the least.'[119] Even those who are blessed with intelligence have their flaws:

> There is another sort of man whom nature has enriched with the full measure of ability and to whom she shows an easy way to come at truth. Among these, even granting inequality in the strength of their ability, there is nevertheless not the same virtue or will in all for the cultivation of their natural sense through practice and learning.[120]

Hugh of Saint-Victor prized natural ability but did not see it as the real virtue that a good student must possess. Academic success could only ever be won by the combination of mental astuteness and hard work. Nothing could be achieved without effort, no matter how intelligent the individual was.

Medieval pedagogical treatises acknowledged the variety of ways in which the process of teaching and the acquisition of knowledge had to take place. In the medieval mind, there was a clear and subtle understanding that one single method of teaching did not work. The presentation of information and the manner in which pupils were persuaded to absorb it had to be different for each child if the process of education was to succeed. While the idea of teaching method depicted in these treatises is, of course, a hypothetical one, it certainly suggests that the medieval classroom was a dynamic place. These treatises expressed the desire for teachers who thought about how they approached each one of their pupils, and that the needs of the individual child had a place in medieval education.

VI
Morals and Religion

TEACHING RELIGION AND MORALS PLAYED A MAJOR role in education in the Middle Ages. Education was always viewed — by theorists, at any rate — as more than a vocational activity. In the modern world, we are encouraged to see formal education as a means to gain academic skills that can be put to work in the wider community, usually for economic benefit. For ancient and medieval thinkers, it was far more than this, more than learning to read and write, more than reading classic works of literature, and more than preparing for a specific set of careers. Instead, the actual process was valued in and of itself. Presenting children with appropriate texts and having them experience the rigours of classroom discipline was seen by commentators as a way to develop cultural norms in children. There were two sides to this attitude:

❖ Firstly, there was the idea that the purpose of education was to lead to a good person and

a valuable citizen. Though first discussed by Quintilian in the first century CE, it persisted in Christian educational thought, as preparation to live a good life in order to become a valuable citizen in the kingdom of God.
- ❖ Secondly, in the context of medieval Christendom, moral and religious instruction allowed the pupil to participate in the wider community as a fellow Christian.

Learning to read was only a means to an end. There were two methods recommended in order for a child or youth ultimately to achieve both terrestrial worth and celestial salvation:

- ❖ Firstly, the child was to be taught the fundamental beliefs and basic prayers of the Christian faith. They were to actively contemplate God, Mary, the lives of the saints and the state of their souls within the classroom.
- ❖ Secondly, the texts and literature that they were to be exposed to had to be of an appropriately elevated and moral tone.

However, what was deemed appropriate and moral was a relative thing and a lot of pagan literature was admitted freely. Indeed, morally 'challenging' texts were considered useful in the medieval classroom since they could be used to demonstrate moral lessons. Terence was a common school text, despite some of the more salacious aspects of his plays. His work was seen as exhibiting characteristics (beyond his excellent Latin) that would have been valuable to a boy on the cusp of adulthood. For example, the play *The Self-Tormentor* may have had a prostitute as a central character, but it also addressed themes such as filial obedience, virtuous love, and the renunciation of sensual pleasures. Both Martin Luther and, much later, John Adams, the second president of the United States, extolled the virtues of Terence, with Adams writing to his son (John Quincy Adams, the sixth president of the United States) that: 'Terence is remarkable, for good morals, good taste, and good Latin.'[121] Nevertheless, there was some resistance to the use of antique authors in the education of Christian children. Little Paula and Pacatula were to have no exposure to 'secular' authors whatsoever, and Alexander Neckham explained that many 'grown men' felt that Ovid's *Amores* and *Ars amatoria* should be 'taken out of adolescent hands'.[122] Moral and religious reading material and lessons were integrated into medieval curricula so that, while the pupil was perfecting their grammar and expanding their vocabulary, they would also consciously and subconsciously learn what was moral and immoral, what was holy and impious.[123]

In some ways it can be argued that a third method for training a holy and useful child was recognised by medieval writers. This was the idea that the process of instruction itself (submission to a master, the self-discipline of learning) was beneficial to the moral state of the pupil's soul. Hugh of Saint-Victor was the principal exponent of this concept. Discipline was one of the three things necessary for those who study, according to Hugh:

> By discipline is meant that, by leading a praiseworthy life, [students] must combine moral behaviour with their knowledge.[124]

This moral and intellectual discipline, acquired in the classroom, was also advocated by Vincent of Beauvais in the introductory chapter of his *On the Education of Noble Children*, where he meditated on Ecclesiasticus 7:25: 'Have you sons? Instruct them and bend their neck from childhood'. While Vincent's views on corporal punishment have already been discussed, it is clear that he saw the process of learning and discipline as essential to forming a moral person.

***

Since moral and religious development was seen by antique and medieval authors as central to any education, the evolution of this idea should be considered. From Quintilian to Vincent of Beauvais, the discussions of citizenship and Christian humility hold in common the idea that education prepared the moral fibre and the soul of the pupil as much as their academic strength of the mind. Quintilian, however, was intent on displaying the value of the instruction that he offered in terms of social responsibility:

> I would not have my orator a philosopher, since no other group of men has withdrawn farther from the duties of citizenship and from all the tasks of oratory. Which of the

> philosophers, indeed, has ever attended assiduously in the law-courts or won fame in public assemblies? Which of them has had practical experience of the administration of public affairs about which most of them are fond of lecturing us? The Roman I am training ought to be wise indeed but one who will prove his worth as a true citizen not in private discussion and debate but by practical experience and exertion.[125]

An active life as a citizen was much better for Rome than the passive contemplations of philosophers, who were viewed — by Quintilian at least — as having little worth to society. This perspective was difficult to apply in early Christian commentaries on education. While Quintilian's pupils were preparing themselves for almost gladiatorial roles in the realm of politics and law, those advised by Jerome were preparing to become citizens of the kingdom of God:

> If you will send us Paula, [...] I shall take more pride in my task than did the worldly philosopher; for I shall not be teaching a Macedonian king, destined to die by poison in Babylon, but a handmaid and bride of Christ who one day shall be presented to the heavenly throne.[126]

But both were being made ready for some sort of service, whether to God or to the *res publica*, and this was the primary objective of education for both Quintilian and Jerome. Augustine, however, was keenly aware that these goals could collide. While Jerome's Paula had been set aside from birth as a handmaid and bride of Christ, Augustine had been trained to live the active life of Quintilian's good citizen, at much expense to his father and after much effort on his own part.[127] In the fourth century, though, the desire to be a good Christian and the wish to be successful in the world were not seen as being compatible, at least by Augustine. He describes his studies as 'empty' and the time he spent as a teacher of rhetoric as a period when 'we went on being led astray and leading others astray', doing 'this publicly, through teaching the subjects which are referred to as "the liberal arts" and privately, under the false name of religion'.[128] Though it was already agreed that study was a way to learn about salvation and to contemplate God (through the Scriptures, especially), Augustine seems to indicate that it was not possible to learn Christian morals via the standard curriculum of late Rome. He contradicts himself, though, when he accepts the importance certain pagan authors had in developing his own approach to God. For example, he writes that reading Cicero's lost work *Hortensius* 'changed the whole feeling of my mind, giving a new direction to the prayers I offered to You, O God'.[129] He also admits that there are elements of truth in pagan authors:

> Any statements by those who are called philosophers, especially the Platonists, which happen to be true and consistent with our

> faith should not cause alarm, but be claimed
> for our own use.[130]

In other words, there is Truth and there are truths, and while minor truths couldn't replace the central Truth, they could still help the student become a better Christian. Augustine's struggle between his training as a rhetor and his upbringing as a Christian is a good example of the blending of classical and Christian concepts — as well as classical and Christian works of literature — in medieval elementary and grammar curricula.[131]

***

In the fourteenth and fifteenth centuries, the primary texts for learning to read were almost all of an explicitly religious nature, but there were exceptions such as Cato's *Distiches*, Aesop's fables, and the *Ilias Latina*, a contracted Latin version of Homer's *Iliad*. Elementary readers were made up of prayers, Psalms, and other devotional items, such as the seven deadly sins and the seven virtues. This tradition was established early on by Augustine and Jerome, who were engaged in forming a Christian curriculum, or rather, a curriculum that could be studied by Christians, educating them and grounding them in their faith at the same time. However, works such as Aesop's fables (a favourite reader of Quintilian's) and, especially, the *Distiches* of Cato continued to be used in both elementary and grammar instruction in the Middle Ages. Ancient writers were frequently included in medieval curricula because they were seen as the best examples of Latin composition. Furthermore, Roman morals were often seen as being compatible with medieval, Christian mores.

In Jerome's letter to Laeta, the Psalms are presented as an ideal teaching tool for a young child, probably because they retained something of their original Hebrew metrical qualities and were therefore easier to memorise.[132] The Psalms were the key introductory reading text from at least the sixth century, where they initially appeared alongside, and then replaced, the *Distiches* of Cato. By repeatedly copying the Psalms on wax tablets, pupils learned to read, to form the letters of the alphabet into words and sentences, and to memorise the sacred text simultaneously. There is no mention of the prayers that would be recommended by some later commentators. Those who do not mention prayers as the elementary text in their programmes do not mention alternatives. It is likely that the use of prayers in this manner was common practice. Philippe of Navarre states clearly that the first lessons taught to children by their parents should be the common prayers of the Middle Ages:

> The first thing that one ought to teach a child, after he begins to believe and listen, so that it is belief in God: the *Credo in Deum, Pater noster, Ave Maria*.[133]

This is repeated by Pierre Dubois, who doesn't shun the use of prayers and Psalms as the initial introduction to reading, placing the Psalms before Cato and the other minor authors but concurrent with 'Donatus' as befitted his accelerated curriculum.[134] Gerson, in his *A.B.C. for Simple People*, translates into French the prayers that were generally used for teaching reading and presents them to his audience of 'boys and girls, big and little' as a catechism and simple reader combined.[135] Aeneas Silvius Piccolomini, writing later in the fifteenth century for the would-be king of Hungary, also expects that his young patron would have begun his own education with prayers and the articles of faith.[136]

The standardisation of advice regarding introductory readings emphasised strongly one aspect of the mentality behind medieval education. These writers lived in Christendom and wanted children to be trained as active members of the Christian community. If children were going to be taught how to read, why not recommend the prayers and beliefs that would bind them into that society and permit them to participate in one of its major communal activities, Christian worship? In this way, even the most rudimentary instruction would allow for this. Furthermore, these Latin texts served as a springboard into grammar education proper for those fortunate enough to continue.

The contents of a medieval child's reader became a part of their daily instructional experience. Prayers and other devotional pursuits were supposed to make up a part of the school day, every day. John of Salisbury described how Bernard of Chartres used moral material in his teaching and set aside the end of the evening revision for prayer:

> Since, however, it is not right to allow
> any school or day to be without religion,

> subject matter was presented to foster faith, build up morals, and to inspire those present at this quasi collation to perform good works. This [evening] 'declination', or philosophical collation, closed with the pious commendation of the souls of the departed to their Redeemer by the devout recitation of the Sixth Penitential Psalm and the Lord's Prayer.[137]

This idea that 'no school or day [should] be without religion' is repeated in Jean Gerson's precepts for the choirboys of Notre Dame in Paris. These boys were required to recite the hours of Our Lady on a daily basis, either in pairs or with the master in charge, as well as frequent trips to confession.[138] These two groups of pupils, however, were clerics of a sort and dedicated already to a life of prayer. But children preparing for secular life also prayed as part of their school day and it is likely that prayers were said on a frequent basis within the schoolroom in order to preserve them in the pupil's memory. Piccolomini expects Prince Ladislas to have learned 'everything that befits a Christian', that is, the *Pater noster*, the *Ave Maria*, the Gospel of John, the Creed, several collects, the mortal sins, the 'Gifts of the Holy Spirit', the Ten Commandments, the 'Works of Mercy', and so on. He does not explicitly state that the prince would have recited these daily but they had to be known so that they could be repeated at any point.[139] Much of what Piccolomini assumes that Ladislas has been taught by way of prayers is the same as what Gerson translates into French in his *A.B.C. for Simple People*, namely the *Pater noster*, the *Ave Maria*, the *Credo*, the Ten Commandments, and selections of church teachings, such as the seven mortal sins and the seven sacraments.[140] The advice given by Gerson and Piccolomini was not for future clerics. They expressed the assumption that all children who had received elementary instruction would know their prayers and the principal articles of their faith. Such recommendations also underline that such an outcome was one of the main goals of such instruction.

As pupils moved from elementary prayers to the grammar curriculum proper, there was a concern that the literature that they were being exposed to was appropriate and articulated, if not Christian ideals, at least compatible moral examples. The compromise regarding the earlier part of the grammar curriculum gradually came into being as the *auctores octo*, or the eight authors. The grammar curriculum in later medieval Europe was relatively standardised across political, cultural, and linguistic borders. While there was no firm definition of which works made up the *auctores octo*, the following works appear to have been the most popular and most widespread:

- ❖ The *Distiches*, a selection of proverbs ascribed to Cato but most likely from third- or fourth-century Spain
- ❖ *Eclogue of Theodulus*, an anonymous tenth-century poem describing a versification competition between the personifications of Truth and the Liar
- ❖ *Tobias*, a verse book on morality from around 1185,

attributed to Matthew of Vendôme, but certainly from France
- ❖ *Doctrinale altum parabolarum*, a collection of proverbs also from France, attributed to Alain de Lille (d. 1204)
- ❖ *De contemptu mundi* (also known as the *Chartula*), a twelfth-century verse treatise on morality once thought to be a work of Bernard of Clairvaux
- ❖ *Facetus*, a verse book on manners and etiquette from early thirteenth-century England, attributed to John of Garland
- ❖ *Liber Aesopi*, available in many Latin editions but the most popular in the later Middle Ages appears to have been its rendering by Gualterus Anglicus (chaplain to Henry II) in the second half of the twelfth century
- ❖ *Floretus*, an anonymous undated religious poem

These *auctores octo* would have poised no problems to the attentive commentator. Most were solidly Christian in their cultural background and the exceptions, such as the *Distiches* of Cato and Aesop's fables, were perfectly moral and upright in tone in addition to being models of good Latin composition.

So while Jerome sought to cut Paula off from any kind of literature that was not explicitly Christian, the existence of the *auctores octo* demonstrates that later teachers and theorists did not have the same qualms. Later authors did not feel it necessary to prevent pupils from being exposed to morally compatible and high quality pagan literature. Vincent of Beauvais has no issue with pagan literature, as long as it is used selectively and with caution. Quoting Jerome (who contradicts his precepts for Paula), he writes:

> We are accustomed, when we read the philosophers, when books of worldly knowledge come into our hands, if we discover anything useful in them, we adapt it to our doctrine. However, if [we discover] anything remaining concerning idols, love, things concerning worldly cares, these we erase.[141]

Vincent goes on to add that even the Bible advocates reading widely: 'Examine everything, hold fast to that which is good' (1 Thessalonians 5:21). Likewise, the author of the *Commendation of the Clerk* felt that texts of both a 'moral character' and 'poetic deduction' should be combined to offer grammar pupils edifying examples and decently-composed Latin.[142] This interplay between good morals and literary quality is also discussed by Gerson and Piccolomini and leads to the idea that, if children were to be prepared properly for this world and the next, they had to be exposed to some writings giving advice on temporal subjects.

In 1417, Gerson wrote a letter to the Dauphin's tutor, which contained a reading list for the prince.[143] Of the thirty-six books that Gerson recommended, twenty are explicitly religious and sixteen are historical, philosophical, and political works, written by both pagans and Christians. The last selection includes books that promote good government, such as Pseudo-Aristotle's *Economics*, Aristotle's *Nicomachean Ethics* and *Politics*, and those that would develop the prince's military knowledge, like Frontinus's *De stratagematibus bellicis* (On the Strategies of War) and Vegetius's *De re militari* (On Military Matters). These were written by pagan authors but they do not gainsay the tenets of Christianity. Their presence in such a list composed for a future ruler is both obvious and sensible. However, the volume of meditative Christian literature recommended by Gerson is impressive. Gerson expects the young prince to spend as much time reading for the next world, no doubt in order to improve his behaviour in this one. This morality and religiosity were essential to becoming and being a good king:

> If the instruction of any boy in religion and virtues is praiseworthy and right, although folly has been bound up in his heart and his feeling and thinking are prone to evil, who does not see how much more praiseworthy beyond the measure of merit it would be to urge this in the case of a son of a king who is expected to be about to rule and about to guide the government or helm of the ship of state of the classes of the whole republic?[144]

While Gerson included the Bible in the course of religious and virtuous instruction, he also suggests a selection of his own works including treatises on such matters as the art of dying well, the Ten Commandments, the examination of conscience and several works concerned with just governance. Of additional interest is the fact that Gerson recommends that many of these works be read in French, rather than Latin. This includes all the works of the *octo auctores*, which were supposed to serve as introductions to Latin reading in the medieval curriculum. This leads us to the realisation that the worth of the *octo auctores* extended beyond their linguistic value and to their worth as vectors of moral and cultural knowledge.[145]

In comparison, Piccolomini's suggested reading in his treatise for Prince Ladislas, written in the early 1450s, reflects the trends of the Italian city states. Gerson's staid diet of devotional essays with minimal exposure to pre-Christian poetry appears odd when examined side-by-side with Piccolomini's *On the Education of Boys*. While Prince Ladislas must believe and must be properly instructed in his faith, the literature that he should concentrate on is far more 'secular':

> Not only the Bible but also pagan literature shows [salvation].[146]

The works of Homer and Virgil (which Piccolomini, in his optimism, recommends as first readers for the young Ladislas) are seen as beneficial not simply because of the 'sublimity of heroic verse' but because the child would be 'endowed with the noblest sentiments'. This is a direct quote from Quintilian.[147] He was struggling, however, against less 'fashionable' feelings about what an education should consist of, especially with regards to poetry. He suggests that some people would object its inclusion in a curriculum:

> Soon, however, the throng of those who wish to seem, rather than be theologians will revile me because I am about to speak of the poets and urge the reading of them. 'Why do you bring poets to us from Italy,' they will say, 'and why do you hasten to corrupt the holy morals of Germany with the effeminate licentiousness of the poets? Was not Marcus Nobilior branded as shameful by your Romans for bringing the poet Ennius into Aetolia when he was consul? Did not your Cicero, whom you follow, whom you admire, say in his *Tusculan Disputations* that the poets were rightly banished by Plato from his imaginary state, since he required the best morals and the best condition for his republic? What about Boethius? Did he not call the Muses of the poets "prostitute actresses"? What about blessed Jerome? Does he not relate that he was beaten by an angel because he was eagerly pursuing profane learning? Depart from us and take your poets with you.'[148]

Yet Piccolomini refuses to accept these arguments (or return to Italy as he feels his detractors would demand) and presents Jerome as the perfect example of the melding of Christian belief and profane education:

> Jerome overflows everywhere with poetic language, nor is there a single line of his that does not smack of Ciceronian eloquence, even though he denied himself Cicero and the odd pagan book. I would say the same of the other doctors of the Church, whose smooth tongues, which would otherwise have been mute, were polished by the poets.[149]

Piccolomini might as well have quoted directly from Augustine's praise of the eloquence of Cicero in helping him to form his prayers to God.[150] Poetry was an issue for some commentators on medieval elementary and grammar education. For example, Gerson excludes all poetry except the moralising verse dialogue of the *Eclogue of Theodulus*.[151] Gerson's recommendations are very extreme, given that Ovid, Terence, Virgil, and Horace (amongst others) were all frequently used by contemporary grammar teachers. And Piccolomini accepts that some poetry is unsuitable for boys to read:

> We do not, indeed, lay it down as a principle that all poets should be read and that boys should study them obsessively. There are many erotic and vicious things in them.[152]

This approach allowed for the maximum exposure of grammar pupils to the finer literature of ancient Rome while protecting them from inappropriate influences. In reality, however, grammar boys were often introduced to more worldly works, like Ovid's *Ars Amatoria* (The Art of Love).[153] Occasionally, this lead to a backlash against the use of all types of pagan literature. Giovanni Dominici, for example, railed against the use of pagan literature in the instruction of a Christian in his educational treatise from around 1400:

> But children of this present age are brought up so that renegade nature is enfeebled in the lap of infidelity, in the midst of reprehensible acts, already soliciting impotent nature to sin; and are taught every infamous evil that can be imagined in the study of all of Ovid, his letters, his *De Arte Amandi*, his most meretricious and carnal writings. Thus they pass through Virgil, the tragedies and other works, teaching them more to love according to the flesh than showing them good morals.[154]

But such debates serve to underline the centrality of the moral and religious character of medieval education. A boy might learn how to compose beautiful Latin but if his soul was condemned to eternal damnation, then the medieval educational process — as envisioned by the majority of pedagogical writers — had failed.

VII
Being a Teacher

> A teacher is understood to be learned,
> stern, mature in age, and neither
> negligent or arrogant.[155]

ACCORDING TO MEDIEVAL EDUCATIONAL THEORISTS, the role of the teacher was diverse, extending beyond their basic purpose of imparting knowledge to their pupils. Their academic responsibility had to be joined with a role as a moral authority and as an example. This was often combined with the idea of the teacher as a pastoral figure, caring for their charges' health and well-being. These functions could change depending on the actual position that a teacher might hold within a school. Most of the literature that dwells on the suitability and character of teachers is exceptionally aspirational, oftentimes declaring that, in order to be a master, one had to be a perfect man. Vincent of Beauvais demands the following:

> Five things are required in a teacher, namely, a clever mind, an honest life, humble

knowledge, unaffected eloquence, and a practical knowledge of teaching.[156]

This list can be reduced to two key topics, the academic character of masters and their moral character. Authors demanded high standards in both since these represented the dual role of the master: that of a teacher and that of a moral example and carer. While the importance placed on moral instruction in medieval educational treatises has already been discussed, it needs to be briefly reexamined in the context of the office of the master.

The principal duty, indeed, the reason for being, of a teacher was as a conduit for academic knowledge. In terms of medieval elementary and grammar curricula, this would have comprised of instructing children in the alphabet, prayers, reading, writing, grammar, rhetoric, and sometimes more. While of course such instruction was the job of the master or multiple masters, it was rarely described by commentators. Indeed, once a discussion of a favoured curriculum had taken place, authors did not feel the need to enumerate the exact academic tasks that a teacher was to complete.[157] There are few hints about what level of education a prospective master was supposed to achieve. It is naturally suggested that ideal teachers should themselves have been educated from a young age. For example, Dubois does not discuss what kind of teachers his young crusaders should have but he does recommend that certain of the graduates should themselves be retained as teachers. In his idealised scheme, some students were never destined to be sent to the Holy Land and were to be trained from childhood to be teachers, especially those who excelled in languages (in this case, Greek, Arabic, and Chaldean).[158] Girls who were delicate but who performed well in subjects like medicine, surgery, and pharmacy were also to be retained as teachers.[159] This emphasis on having thoroughly educated masters and mistresses who had long experience as pupils before moving on to teaching was not always played out in reality, however. With regards to titles and 'professional' qualifications, there is an acceptance that a person did not necessarily need to have a degree in order to be a competent teacher. The anonymous author of the *Commendation* spends a certain amount of time considering this subject. For him, there are four types of masters:

> For one man is a master in title and reality, another in reality but not in title, a third in title but not in reality, a fourth neither in title nor reality but in name only.[160]

The first is, of course, favoured, but the second, the master without title but with the learning and experience, is still an honourable man:

> The master in reality but not in title is he who has the treasure of science and the heritage of virtue but does not have a privileged title. And he is like a noble, strong and praiseworthy in arms, who has not yet been knighted.[161]

The last two are described in unfavourable terms as counterfeiters who seek the style and privileges of the office without undergoing the tests and depredations of training. While these descriptions are applied to masters of Arts, the author considers the question of title versus ability in the case of more elementary schoolmasters:

> And first concerning schools where often not a master in arts presides but a teacher of boys is named without title, who however sometimes is really a master although he lacks the title.[162]

Title and diplomas are not required but can serve as a means to judge when someone has received the requisite instruction themselves. But a teacher with neither title nor ability is dubbed a 'vainglorious' leader.[163] Perhaps this is why so little attention is given to this in pedagogical literature. The emphasis is clearly on whether a person is capable and knowledgeable rather than a graduate of a great university. Neither Gerson nor Philippe of Navarre nor Piccolomini nor any of the others state explicitly what kind of formal training a would-be teacher should have. Gerson's only stipulation regarding the masters of the choirboys of Paris is that the song master 'should be of such morals as to be destined to be the master we name.'[164] This brings us to the qualification that pedagogical commentators really focused their attentions on: the moral standing of the master.[165]

In his treatise *On Christian Doctrine*, Augustine defines the impetus behind the focus on the morality of a teacher:

> No matter how impressive the style of a speaker, his life has the greater influence in ensuring that his audience is receptive to his words. For the man who speaks wisely and eloquently but who leads a wicked life, may indeed teach many who are eager to learn, although, as it is written, 'he is unprofitable to his own soul.' (Ecclesiasticus 37:12)[166]

The centrality of this idea, that a moral man would have a more important impact on his students than an immoral man, is reflected in later literature; indeed this idea is a key tenet of medieval pedagogical commentary. Let us consider this in the case of Gerson's recommendations regarding the choirboys at Paris. These boys were precious, especially considering their role in the divine offices of the Church. As servants of God, they had to be protected. The master, therefore, had to be uncorrupted and untainted 'because what will the student do if not that which he sees the master doing'.[167] They were not to be exposed to any kind of inappropriate behaviour. Indeed, they were neither to see evil nor hear it:

> No one should sin before his eyes, neither by repulsive and obscene word, nor by a deceitful and dissolute gesture or touch, nor by a wanton and evil deed.[168]

While the master of the boys was a focus for such exhortations, the master of grammar was also required to be of impeccable character. He too was to be 'of such morals, which we have said the [master of the boys] ought to have'.[169] Clearly, the moral nature of the job was just as important if not more important than the academic one. The statement that the grammar teacher should be of high moral fibre is made before any discussion of his role in the classroom. Indeed, Gerson does not make any demands regarding the teacher's intellectual formation or expertise. In addition, either the master of the boys or the master of grammar had to be with the boys all the time:

> And both should arrange the hours of the day and the night in such a manner that always one of them can attend to the boys, in the house as well as outside in whatever place the boys happen to go.[170]

The reason for this was three-fold. Firstly, they were there to protect the boys. Gerson is very keen to ensure that the boys were isolated to a certain extent from those outside the cathedral school. This is almost certainly because of the fear of unsavoury characters taking advantage of the boys:

> In addition servants should be forbidden from having close friendship with them, indeed those not of the household nor clerics nor servants nor chaplains should not be tolerated to consort with them

particularly unless in the presence of one of
the masters.[171]

Gerson describes this in terms of one bad sheep leading the flock astray. Secondly, they were to supervise the behaviour of the boys. Gerson is exhaustive in describing the sins that should be watched for and corrected in the boys, from speaking French to chattering in church.[172] Thirdly, they were there to act as examples. The masters were meant to be living illustrations of the highest standards of behaviour and had to be constantly exhibited to their pupils. Just as bad habits could be formed by observation, so too could good habits. While the teachers watched the boys, the boys watched them, combining learning with childish imitation. In the medieval teacher, as in the medieval curriculum, morality and academic attainment went hand-in-hand.

While commentators focused on the propriety of teachers and only made passing remarks on the academic qualifications necessary, there is some discussion on the roles and specialties of a master in terms of a school's hierarchy. As we have seen above, Gerson's choir school was to have a master (*magister, magister puerorum*) and a master of grammar (*magister grammaticae*). The first was in charge of the school, the boys, and the other teachers. In many ways, he resembled a type of headmaster, more concerned with administration and discipline rather than actual instruction. The grammar teacher taught the boys Latin language and grammar, in addition to acting as an assistant to the master of the boys. Added to these personnel was the figure of the song master (*magister cantus*) who taught the boys singing, music, and the liturgical repertory necessary to their position:

> Let the master of song teach the boys at set hours, principally full chant and counterpoint, and other worthy descants, not dissolute and shameless refrains, nor should he press them so much in such things that they ruin progress in grammar.[173]

Gerson does not assign the song master any particular supervisory role over the boys. In this organisational format, there were three masters in the school, only two of whom had the responsibility of guardianship. While Gerson does not make any comment on the matter, one wonders if either the master or the grammar master had to be present with the boys during their singing lessons.

This hierarchy can be directly compared to that recommended by the author of the *Commendation*. In the 'illegitimate school house of the artists' (that is, the average grammar school whose principal is either not a master at all or who has a degree from a university 'of slight reputation lacking privileges from princes of the world'), there were four officers.[174] The first is the master who was the *paterfamilias* of the school. Secondly there was the disciple who appears to be a type of trainee-master. The master's relationship to the disciple was compared to the relationship between a father and his heir, to whom he 'dispenses the treasures of his mind or at least tries to'.[175] Thirdly there was the pedagogue who helps the boys in the classroom like a kind of assistant. Finally there is the monitor, who observed the boys and noted down their mistakes and transgressions. It is clear that this was a relatively low-level school catering to younger boys who required more help in the course of their lessons and more constraints on their behaviour — as the author himself states explicitly:

> Assistants are more opportune in unlicensed schools of artists than in others, because their hordes are younger and more heterogeneous and so require more tutors in acquiring both morals and knowledge.[176]

This is in comparison to the 'authentic' schools where, apart from janitors and bedels, there are only three officers; the master, the disciple, and the bachelor (who acts as a substitute for the master).[177] Even though, in reality, most schools were made up of a single teacher giving lessons to a broad range of children learning at different levels, those with more complicated organisations did resemble the patterns laid down by Gerson and the anonymous author of the *Commendation* and were directly paralleled in towns and cities across medieval Europe. The many roles that the master was supposed to play in the medieval schoolroom indicated the position's theoretical sophistication in the eyes of commentators. While the academic requirements for the job may have been passed over or taken for granted, the interest in the character of the master emphasises their function as guardian and model, and underlines the task of education to form the personality of the pupil as well as the mind.

VIII
Education of Women

WOMEN AND GIRLS ARE GENERALLY NOT SEEN AS BEING the traditional recipients of education — even of elementary and grammar education — in the Middle Ages. There is a tendency to ascribe misogynistic attitudes to theoretical literature on education without fully comprehending the nature of some treatises. For example, in Gerson's *For the Boys of the Church of Paris*, there is no mention or discussion of the instruction of girls. This, of course, is completely appropriate as the treatise is directed at a specific group, in this case, choirboys. There is no discussion of the education of girls in Quintilian's *Education of an Orator* because this is aimed at the professional training of orators and other public men. Hugh of Saint-Victor does not examine female education either in the *Didascalicon* since this work was a weighty and oftentimes abstract consideration of the nature of knowledge, without any explicitly gender-based motivation. However, none of these works necessarily represented any real opposition to girls participating in formal intellectual development in the classroom. In other writings, Gerson, for example, spoke directly to girls as his audience:

> Listen all, little and big, boys and girls, and other simple people.[178]

Though women could not become orators in first-century Rome, Quintilian still discussed the importance of having an engaged and educated mother for the future success of her sons:

> As to parents, I should wish them to be as highly educated as possible. (I do not mean only the fathers. We are told that the eloquence of the Gracchi owed much to their mother Cornelia, whose highly cultivated style is known also to posterity from her letters).[179]

The education of women was frequently discussed in a great deal of detail by medieval authors, but we must be careful not to see the absence of such discussion as direct opposition to the intellectual development of women. Instead, the focus of this chapter will be those treatises that explicitly examine the how and why of female education, and both the positive and negative ways in which it was viewed by commentators.

It can be argued that the pedagogical literature concerning girls had a greater emphasis on morals than that for boys. According to Rosemary Barton Tobin in her book on women in Vincent of Beauvais, the education of women is not physical, only partially intellectual, but almost completely moral in its aims in the Middle Ages.[180] As we saw above, the education of all children in the Middle Ages was intensely moral and religious. Indeed, since that was seen by many theorists as being the central rationale for any instruction, it is difficult to construct a discourse based on gendered differentiation. It is also problematic to suggest that such a moral focus was more pertinent for girls than, for example, for boys who were preparing for clerical careers during which they were supposed to have the care of souls. Of course, it was a factor, and a strong factor, in the educational experience of girls and cannot be ignored. However, it should always be viewed in the wider context of medieval pedagogical trends.

The education of girls was just another part of medieval instruction that authors had to consider and was not a rare, unusual, or monstrous thing. Vincent of Beauvais seems to emphasise that girls should be completely virtuous and suggests that this trait must already be in place before any education begins. Quoting Ovid, he wrote:

> No one is able to acquire knowledge
> If he offends modesty.[181]

While he cited this at the beginning of his chapters on the education of women, he had already spent a great deal of time discussing the need to engender sufficient goodness and right living in the sons of nobles. What is of interest here is that he suggested that an excellent moral state of being is required in girls *before* they begin to learn, while morality and goodness may be developed during the education of boys:

> As long as noble girls are kept safe by the aforementioned diligent rule of parents, it is suitable that they should be imbued in letters and instructed in morals.[182]

The girl must be good and made secure *before* she is made better through education. Vincent of Beauvais, however, seems to turn this point on its head a few pages later. He himself did not necessarily see that he had made a distinction between moral prerequisites for boys and for girls:

> Because again it has been said above concerning boys, the same should be encouraged in the immature period of life of girls, that they should be evidently instructed in morals and good habits.[183]

For Vincent, moral instruction was absolutely necessary for both boys and girls. Perhaps his focus on this subject in these chapters pertaining to girls and women was simply because he had already discussed his course of intellectual education and believed that what was recommended for the sons of nobles was just as applicable for their daughters. Perhaps he felt that he would have been repeating himself if he had examined what should be taught and what should be read all over again. It is difficult to say for certain, especially with Vincent of Beauvais, whether morality is discussed because it was simply a part of medieval education or whether writers wanted to underline its importance for women.

The creation of a protective cocoon around a female pupil as part of their education, as advocated by Vincent of Beauvais, may initially seem to be gender-specific. The emphasis on keeping the girl safe and secure and ensuring that her innate, pre-existing, goodness not be tarnished in any way, has a long tradition. Jerome demands the same for Paula:

> She must have no comprehension of foul words, no knowledge of worldly songs, and her childish tongue must be imbued with the sweet music of the Psalms. Let boys with their wanton frolics be kept far from Paula: let even her maids and attendants hold aloof from association with the worldly, lest they render their evil knowledge worse by teaching it to her.[184]

But these demands should not necessarily be interpreted as being inherently misogynistic or paternalistic. Vincent of Beauvais is just as concerned with the morals of his noble boys as well as his noble girls. And Jean Gerson's recommendations for the choirboys of Paris in order to keep them safe and pure and innocent of the tawdry nature of the world around them are very like Jerome's recommendations for Paula:

> We do not wish that anyone should be admitted intending to stay with the boys nor to learn with them from outside, unless by special license of the superiors, lest our boys get bad habits from intimacy with others, for a single bad sheep corrupts every sheep, especially where anyone had been bent and introduced to immense sins which ought not even to be named.[185]

These fears appear particularly appropriate when we remember that both Paula and the choirboys were in training for lives of religious and clerical celibacy and service. But such fears also permeate the advice for boys who would become men of the world. Piccolomini had no wish for the young king of Hungary to be surrounded by those who would lead him astray:

> For this reason let those who assist you be instructed in good morals; let there be no vice in them; let them employ no foul language, for we are all prone to imitate shameful and corrupt ways [...] 'Habit is strong in tender years', as Virgil says.[186]

The strong emphasis on maintaining morals in pupils, going so far as to isolate them from the unsavoury influence of the rowdy lads down the street, is the same for both boys and girls.

Virtue and good morals, however, had to be sustained during the course of a girl's education, as in a boy's.

This was done in more ways than reading religious and edifying literature. As Vincent of Beauvais suggests, reading should be joined with prayer and work.[187] The practice of prayer is present in almost all the pedagogical treatises mentioned here, with the *Pater noster*, *Credo*, and *Ave Maria* being the first things that elementary pupils learned. But for girls, working with the hands was seen as a particularly important part of their education. There is no mention of boys doing any sort of craft or manual work in the educational treatises of the Middle Ages — with the notable example of Dubois's crusading builders with their weaponised mirrors. It is here, therefore, that we see a marked departure in the recommendations for boys and for girls. Girls had to be kept busy with work when not actively being instructed. Then again, boys also engaged in physical, non-academic activities as part of their education. Boys who were preparing for active lives in the realms of politics and war were, of course, encouraged to train as soldiers and partake in other knightly pursuits, such as hunting. Piccolomini references Vegetius's *De re militari* (On Military Matters) several times in his recommendations to Ladislas of Hungary, for example, urging him to learn military skills and 'to acquire strong and well-knit limbs'.[188] These activities were not open to girls. Vincent of Beauvais does not state in his own words what 'work' girls were to do but instead quotes heavily from Jerome. Jerome, who in many ways is our most valuable source on the elementary education of girls at the beginning of the Middle Ages, encouraged other, specific activities:

> Let her learn also to make wool, to hold the distaff, to put the basket in her lap, to turn the spindle, to shape the thread with her thumb.[189]

While Roman tradition held such activities as the proper occupation of high-born women, both Jerome and Vincent see it in another light. While secular boys might be out training in arms or riding or learning to hold the reins of state, their sisters were limited to praying and textile work. By learning these more mundane skills, the girls were once again being protected. As Jerome wrote and Vincent of Beauvais quoted:

> Work, so that the devil should always find you occupied.[190]

While girls were assigned the staff over the sword, however, the fear of idleness leading to sin was equally a concern for boys. Jerome's exhortation to work in order to keep the devil at bay was first directed at a brother monk, not at a woman or a girl. It is, therefore, difficult to say with certainty if Jerome and Vincent thought girls particularly vulnerable to the evils of indolence or whether they simply sought an acceptable substitution for the activities open to boys.

What do pedagogical theorists say concerning the actual, intellectual education of girls? The emphasis, of course, was always on learning prayers and reading the Bible, just as it was for their male counterparts. Jerome's course of studies, for example, is completely Christian and almost completely scriptural. Little Paula was to follow her alphabet with singing the Psalms and Proverbs and work her way through the entire Bible until she could 'safely' read the Song of Songs. This reading would be augmented by suitable Christian writers such as Cyprian, Athanasius, and Hilary:

> Then at last she may safely read the Song of Songs: if she were to read it at the beginning she might be harmed by not perceiving it as the song of a spiritual bride expressed in fleshly language.[191]

This was a purely religious education, tailored for a child who was already dedicated as a handmaid of the Lord. Peter Abelard's letter to a group of Paraclete nuns heavily references Jerome's letter to Laeta, demonstrating the Church Father's continued relevance in pedagogical matters.[192] Much of the content does not change over time, even for secular girls in the later Middle Ages. For example, Rosemary Barton Tobin in her work on Vincent of Beauvais and the education of women quotes from a thirteenth-century sermon by Humbert of Romans (d. 1277). He was clear what young girls, especially those who are of a higher social order, were supposed to learn and why:

> Note that these girls, especially if they be the daughters of the rich, ought to devote themselves to study, for to this purpose their parents have intended them. Hence

> they ought to know the Psalter or Hours of Our Lady or the Office of the Dead or other prayers to God, and so be more fitted for religious life should they wish to join it later, or more fitted for the study of Sacred Scripture, like Paula and Eustochia and others who remained unwedded, and because of their devotion to books became deeply versed in sacred letters.[193]

Humbert was unambiguous: girls should be educated only for religious reasons. As a result, if they became nuns they could participate in the liturgy. If they were studious spinsters, they could emulate Jerome's Paula. Other authors responded differently to the question of what to do with an educated girl. In the book written by Geoffrey de la Tour Landry in the fourteenth century, education was to be valued in a marriage. He gives the example of Delbora, a figure from the *Golden Legend*. Her mother sends her to school to learn *clergie* (signifying a Latin education) and Holy Scripture. Her husband is both evil and cruel but, through her good sense and thanks to her education, Delbora is able to change him into a good ruler:

> Therefore this is a good example of how one must put one's daughters to learning the wisdom of the clergy and Holy Scripture; because if they are knowing they can better see their salvation and better recognise evil from good.[194]

This is echoed by Vincent of Beauvais when he wrote that a wife 'should neither be a mistress nor a servant, but a companion'.[195] Even basic instruction in Latin literature would allow for a husband and wife to interact on a somewhat more equal level. Such instruction would also allow girls to read beyond their psalms and books of hours. However, while exposure to the correct material enabled girls to 'avoid harmful thoughts and avoid the pleasures of the flesh', more worldly fare would lead them astray.[196] De la Tour Landry warns against books of 'lecheries' or 'worldly fables' as they simply offer no profit to their readers.[197] The profit in question was a moral and spiritual one. However, this was very much the case for boys too. They too had to learn their prayers and read their psalms and avoid inappropriate reading material, especially during elementary and the early parts of grammar education. While the message may have been underlined for girls, it was the same message: instruction and education were additional means by which to save one's soul.

Two writers in particular appear to have taken utterly opposite positions on the question of the education of girls. Pierre Dubois, in his *Recovery of the Holy Land*, includes girls in his radical educational scheme from the start. Both boys and girls were to attend his preparation schools, both were to take part in Latin grammar instruction, and there were a range of roles for them when they had completed their studies. Firstly, they could be trained as physicians, surgeons, or apothecaries.

> All the girls of the foundation, like the males, should be instructed in Latin grammar and afterwards in logic and in one foreign language; then in the fundamentals of the natural sciences and finally in surgery and medicine.[198]

Dubois explains the importance of this in the context of a crusade:

> Especially [would they influence] the women whom they would aid through the practice of medicine and surgery, and particularly in their secret infirmities and needs.[199]

Secondly, the most handsome would be given theological training and married to both Greek and Muslim men of importance. They could then act as undercover Christian missionaries.[200] Thirdly, girls who were particularly gifted and who had delicate health could stay at the schools in France as teachers of surgery, medicine, or languages.[201] This was a dizzying plan. For Dubois, everyone had to aid in the retaking of the Holy Land and girls were not to be excused from this duty. Possibly the most radical thing that he suggests is that if girls are bright and responding well to study, they could be exempt from 'the morning canonical hours and the celebration of Masses' in his reformed convent schools.[202] Dubois, for one, clearly felt that gifted girls were too often kept at their prayers when they could be learning and actively contributing to the world at large.

Dubois's views were, of course, highly unconventional and did not reflect the realities of the education of young girls. The strident ideas of Philippe of Navarre regarding their education took an entirely opposing position. More than any other author, Navarre pleads for the limitation of girls' intellectual development. For him, girls should not be taught to read or to write at all, unless they were to become nuns:

> A woman must not learn to read and write,
> unless especially to become a nun, because
> by reading and writing a woman becomes
> evil.[203]

Reading and writing would lead to the sending and receiving of love letters, to the loss of their complexion, and to the Devil.[204]

Both Dubois and Navarre are extremists in their opinions. While one would have girls skipping Mass to attend lessons and working as physicians and surgeons, the other would have them remain wholly ignorant for their own good. As has already been demonstrated, neither of these approaches would have been considered wise or appropriate by other pedagogical theorists, but not simply because the pupils in question were girls. Boys, like girls, had to be instructed in a moral way and few went beyond the fundamentals that would allow them to read or follow the liturgy. If either boys or girls went further, they were rarely exposed to controversial literature, and in no way were girls prevented from reading the same pagan literature as their male counterparts. When it came to elementary education in particular, medieval authors did not make a distinction between boys and girls. As a discrete process, standing alone from grammar and university instruction that might (but rarely did) come next, elementary instruction was relatively genderless.

Conclusion

It is abundantly clear from this overview of pedagogical writings that elementary and grammar education was considered a fit topic for contemplation and deliberation by medieval writers. They demonstrated that debates on basic instruction stretched sometimes over centuries, and made for lively discourse between thinkers and even lively reading for the teacher, the parent, and, eventually, for us. Such writings considered how children should be ready to enter into their communities. For able clerical boys, that meant preparing for university studies and a career in the Church. For another, perhaps an apprentice in a town, learning to read, to count, and to write would give him an edge over the competition later in life. For a young girl, elementary education could mean better marriage prospects, the ability to teach her own children, or even to become a schoolmistress in her own right. For each, elementary and grammar education could represent a heightened understanding of Christian teachings. All these writers understood that these were the stakes of elementary and grammar education, and all sought to discover the best means and methods to achieve these goals.

For the modern reader, be they an academic researcher or a more casual explorer of things medieval, classical and medieval pedagogical writings are a treasury of opinions, intellectual disputes, and schoolroom reminiscences that cannot be found in documentary records. These entirely subjective works serve as a backdrop for understanding the nature of medieval elementary and grammar education, lending colour and texture. Without them, we could be fooled into thinking that the medieval approach to education was uniform, unforgiving, and uninventive. Instead, we are aware of the gravity with which serious minds considered the instruction of children. We appreciate the variety of viewpoints. And, most importantly, we can see the subtle understanding and flexibility that writers employed when examining the challenges faced by little pupils and their teachers.

Notes

1 Ariès, *Centuries of Childhood*, 137.
2 *Quintilian on Education*, xxi.
3 This tradition was engrained so early in the Renaissance reception of Quintilian that it appeared in the orator's entry in the Nuremberg Chronicle from 1493, where it is explicitly stated that his work was lost until it was rediscovered by 'Pogio Flore(n)tino' in a monastery. Schedel, *Liber chronicarium*, iii.3.
4 Augustine, *Confessions*, iii, 3–6.
5 *The Colloquies of Ælfric Bata*, 2, 208–09.
6 Dumitrescu, 'The Grammar of Pain in Ælfric Bata's *Colloquies*', 240–43.
7 Searle, *The Terrors of St Trinian's*, and Willans & Searle, *Molesworth*.
8 Since the *Didascalicon* and *Metalogicon* are best known by their Greek titles, I will use them to avoid confusion.
9 John of Salisbury, *Metalogicon*, 67.
10 Some suggest Denmark (based on the popularity of the name 'Boethius' there in the thirteenth century), while others prefer England, based on its early popularity there and its references to other texts common or originating in England. Pseudo-Boethius, *De disciplina scolarium*, 5–8.

11 Pseudo-Boethius, *De disciplina scolarium*, 76 & 79.
12 Philippe of Navarre, *Les Quatres ages*, 10.
13 It is unclear whether Gerson composed these proverbs himself or whether he collected pre-existing sayings. This is certainly an avenue worth further exploration.
14 Lynch, *Elementary and Grammar Education*, 101–02.
15 Fourteen was considered the standard age to begin university in the Middle Ages.
16 Jean Froissart, *Un Galant de douze ans*, 155–56.
17 Fédou, *Les Hommes de loi*, 17.
18 For more on education and literacy in rural areas of France see: Guilbert, 'Les Écoles rurales en Champagne au XVe siècle', 127–47.
19 Chaucer, *The Canterbury Tales*, 160.
20 Chaucer, *The Canterbury Tales*, 161.
21 Willemsen, *Back to the Schoolyard*, 142 & 267.
22 Alexandre-Bidon & Lorcin, *Système éducatif et cultures dans l'Occident medieval*.
23 Alexander Neckham, *Sacerdos ad altare*, 536.
24 For these treatises, see *Humanist Educational Treatises*, edited and translated by Craig Kallendorf.
25 Isidore of Seville, *Etymologies*, XI.ii.1–4.
26 John of Salisbury, *Metalogicon*, (1:24) 68–69.
27 Quintilian, *Institutio*, 1.1.xvi.
28 Quintilian, *Institutio*, 1.1.iv–1.1.xiv.
29 Quintilian, *Institutio*, 1.1.ix.
30 Philippe of Navarre, *Les quatre ages*, 10.
31 Giles of Rome, *Li Livres du gouvernement des rois*, 197.
32 *Commendation of the Clerk*, 211.
33 *Commendation of the Clerk*, 223.
34 Quintilian, *Institutio*, 1.1.xx.

35 Dubois, *Recovery of the Holy Land*, 117.
36 Dubois, *Recovery of the Holy Land*, 135.
37 Dubois, *Recovery of the Holy Land*, 127.
38 It should be noted that these were the boys intended for full university study in theology and medicine: Dubois, *Recovery of the Holy Land*, 128.
39 *Commendation of the Clerk*, 225.
40 The author of *On the Teaching of School* is particularly concerned that teachers and students alike make use of the daylight for their work. Pseudo-Boethius, *De disciplina scolarium*, 126–27.
41 Orme, *Medieval Schools*, 143–44, and Willemsen, *Back to the Schoolyard*, 26.
42 Dubois, *Recovery of the Holy Land*, 126–27.
43 Gerson, 'Pro pueris', IX, 687.
44 Gerson, 'Pro pueris', IX, 687.
45 Gerson, 'Pro pueris', IX, 687. In Pseudo-Boethius's *On the Teaching of School*, it is suggested that morning is the correct time for musical work. Pseudo-Boethius, *On the Teaching of School*, 126–27.
46 Dubois, *Recovery of the Holy Land*, 126.
47 Dubois's proposal that more advanced grammar should be taught during the winter months is also present in the statutes of the University of Toulouse in 1328. Lectures there on the *Doctrinale* and the *Graecismus* were limited to the winter months: *Statuts et* privilèges, I, 501.
48 Dubois, *Recovery of the Holy Land*, 117.
49 John of Salisbury, *Metalogicon*, 1.24 (68).

50 John of Salisbury, *Metalogicon*, 1.24 (70). This type of confabulation also appears in Pseudo-Boethius, but in the afternoon rather than the evening. Pseudo-Boethius, *On the Teaching of School*, 127.

51 Dubois, *Recovery of the Holy Land*, 126.

52 Gerson, 'Pro pueris', IX, 688.

53 John of Salisbury, *Metalogicon*, 1.24 (68).

54 Ælfric Bata, *Colloquies*, 85–87.

55 In the Netherlands, school ended in the late afternoon, at five or six o'clock: Willemsen, *Back to the Schoolyard*, 26.

56 Ælfric Bata, *Colloquies*, 88–91.

57 Orme, *Medieval Schools*, 44–45.

58 Gabriel, *The Educational Ideas of Vincent of Beauvais*, 20.

59 Quintilian, *Institutio*, 1.3.viii.

60 *Commendation of the Clerk*, 225.

61 Gerson, 'Pro pueris', IX, 688.

62 Quintilian, *Institutio*, 1.3.xi.

63 Orme, 'Games and Education', 49. Despite the appearance of cock-fighting in England and in parts of France (see Mehl, *Les Jeux au royaume de France*), there were attempts to curb it. In 1518, for example, it was prohibited at Saint Paul's School in London. Nevertheless, the tradition persisted well into the modern period. Teachers and pupils at Manchester Grammar School seem to have continued to enjoy Shove Tuesday cock-fights until 1815. Parry, *Education in England*, 113.

64 Gerson, 'Pro pueris', IX, 688.

65 It is interesting to note that many writers felt that learning itself should be fun. Quintilian and Jerome felt that the earliest lessons in particular should not be boring and should catch the interest of a small child. 'For one of the first things

to take care of is that the child, who is not yet able to love study, should not come to hate it and retain his fear of the bitter taste he has experienced even beyond his first years. Let it be a game; let him be questioned and praised and always feel glad that he has done something; sometimes, when he refuses a lesson, it should be given to another child, of whom he can be jealous; sometimes he should compete, and more often than not think he is the winner; and finally he should be encouraged by rewards suitable to his age': Quintilian, *Institutio*, 1.1.xx. 'Offer her prizes for spelling, tempting her with such trifling gifts as please young children. Let her have companions too in her lessons, so that she may seek to rival them and be stimulated by any praise they win. You must not scold her if she is somewhat slow; praise is the best sharpener of wits. Let her be glad when she is first and sorry when she falls behind. Above all take care not to make her lessons distasteful; a childish dislike often lasts longer than childhood': Jerome, 'Letter to Laeta', ch. 4. This approach combined learning with play in order to ease the child into the realm of formal schooling.

66 Ælfric Bata, *Colloquies*, 94–95.
67 The general suggestion from the archives in Lyon is that the schoolmaster either used a room in their own abode or rented a separate room or building to hold class.
68 *Commendation of the Clerk*, 223.
69 Willemsen, *Back to the Schoolyard*, 141–43 & 267–68. Orme also gives some information on the location of and nature of schools in later medieval England. For example, some schoolrooms were part of local churches and this caused problems. In 1373, the churches of King's Lynn were forbidden from keeping schools within the same building

'on the grounds that the cries of beaten pupils interrupted services and distracted worshippers.' Orme, *Medieval Schools*, 135–41 (136).

70 There is little information regarding possible decorations in the medieval classroom. However, woodcuts from the sixteenth century depict charts (especially of musical notation) in classrooms: Willemsen, *Back to the Schoolyard*, 267–68. Furthermore, in conversation with Dr Anthony Masinton of the University of York in May 2012, I was informed that restoration projects at Durham had revealed medieval musical notation and liturgical text scratched into the walls of a chapel within the bishop's palace. While I have as yet been unable to verify this independently, it suggests that visual aids were presented to pupils on the walls of the rooms within which they studied.

71 Benedict, *Rule*, ch. XLV (68).

72 *Augustine on Education*, 34–35.

73 *Augustine on Education*, 37.

74 This is part of Augustine's philosophy of pain: that it is omnipresent in the world in order to teach humanity about its damnation and as a means of achieving grace. A thrashing at the hands of a teacher combines the salutary effects of physical punishment with pedagogical benefits: 'For what is the meaning of the manifold threats that are employed to restrain the foolishness of children? What of the attendants, the masters, ferule, the thongs, the rods and that discipline whereby the Holy Spirit says the sides of the beloved son should be beaten, lest he grow up unbroken? For when he is once hardened, he can be tamed with difficulty, or perhaps not at all. What is the purpose of all these penalties, except

to overcome ignorance and restrain base desire, which are evils with which we come into this world?' Augustine, *City of God*, XXII.22.

75 *Augustine on Education*, 36.
76 Vincent of Beauvais, *De eruditione*, 6.
77 Vincent of Beauvais, *De eruditione*, 6.
78 Vincent of Beauvais, *De eruditione*, 6.
79 Vincent of Beauvais, *De eruditione*, 7.
80 Vincent of Beauvais, *De eruditione*, 8. See also Quintilian, *Institutio*, 1.3.xii.
81 Vincent of Beauvais, *De eruditione*, 92.
82 'Likewise it is proper to add a third [aspect], namely discretion, which shall be guarded in these: manner and time and place': Vincent of Beauvais, *De eruditione*, 93.
83 'In the case of manner three things are required, namely good intention and genuine purpose and restraint or measured action': Vincent of Beauvais, *De eruditione*, 93.
84 Vincent of Beauvais, *De eruditione*, 95.
85 Gerson, 'Pro pueris', IX, 688.
86 Vincent of Beauvais, *De eruditione*, 95.
87 Ælfric Bata, *Colloquies*, 164–71. Scholars are uncertain if Ælfric intended this to serve as an example of 'good teaching', a first-person account of activities in an Anglo-Saxon schoolroom, or merely as a 'fun' story to teach pupils the Latin words for various crimes and how to plead for mercy. See Dumitrescu, *The Grammar of Pain*, 239–40.
88 Piccolomini, 138–39. See also Quintilian, *Institutio*, 2.4.x–xi and Vincent of Beauvais, *De eruditione*, 94.
89 Quintilian, *Institutio*, 2.4.x–xi.
90 Piccolomini, 'The Education of Boys', 138–39.
91 Quintilian, *Institutio*, 1.3.xiv.

92 Quintilian, *Institutio*, 1.3.xv.

93 Jerome, *Letter to Laeta*, pt. 4.

94 Quintilian, *Institutio*, 1.3.xiv.

95 Jerome, *Letter to Laeta*, pt. 4.

96 Jerome, *Letter to Pacatula*, pt. 1.

97 Vincent of Beauvais, *De eruditione*, 94.

98 *Commendation of the Clerk*, 225.

99 John of Salisbury, *Metalogicon*, 1.24 (68). Ælfric Bata, whose *Colloquies* are sometimes read as a gruelling exposé of violence in the medieval classroom, suggested moderation in punishment: 'Masters, don't provoke your sons to anger with needlessly harsh sternness, but discipline with moderation and kindness, sometimes rebuking, sometimes reproving, sometimes entreating, and sometimes whipping.' Ælfric Bata, *Colloquies*, 86–87.

100 John of Salisbury, *Metalogicon*, 1.24 (69).

101 Gerson, 'Pro pueris', IX, 688.

102 Dubois, *Recovery of the Holy Land*, 117.

103 Dubois, *Recovery of the Holy Land*, 125.

104 Pseudo-Boethius, *On the Teaching of School*, 99.

105 *Commendation of the Clerk*, 223.

106 Quintilian, *Institutio*, 1.1.i.

107 Ælfric Bata, *Colloquies*, 90–93.

108 *Commendation of the Clerk*, 224. This is clearly based on Pseudo-Boethius's assertion: 'But certain youths are exceedingly obtuse, others are mediocre, and a third are excellently sharp.' Pseudo-Boethius, *On the Teaching of School*, 119.

109 *Commendation of the Clerk*, 225.

110 Quintilian, *Institutio*, 1.3.vi.

111 John of Salisbury, *Metalogicon*, 1.24 (67).

112 John of Salisbury, *Metalogicon*, 1.24 (68).
113 Augustine, *Confessions*, i, 13–14.
114 Dubois, *Recovery of the Holy Land*, 131.
115 Dubois, *Recovery of the Holy Land*, 136.
116 Dubois, *Recovery of the Holy Land*, 137.
117 Hugh of Saint-Victor, *Didascalicon*, 43.
118 In the *Commendation of the Clerk*, the change from the grammar curriculum to the dialectic one was seen as the point when the weaker boys peeled away and the master was left with the brighter pupils: *Commendation of the Clerk*, 225.
119 Hugh of St Victor, *Didascalicon*, 43.
120 Hugh of St Victor, *Didascalicon*, 43–44.
121 McCullough, *John Adams*, 259.
122 Neckham himself does not seem particularly perturbed by the works of Ovid but he does flag an ongoing debate about the suitability of his works in a Christian curriculum. Alexander of Villedieu, for example, denounced the use of Ovid's *Fasti* (a calendar of pagan festivities) in the classroom. It may simply be a coincidence that this denunciation was made at the beginning of Alexander of Villedieu's own work, *Ecclesiale*, a calendar of the Christian year which he clearly was positioning as an appropriate replacement. Alexander Neckham, *Sacerdos ad altare*, 537 & 537, n. 26.
123 Vincent of Beauvais, *De eruditione*, 6–8.
124 Hugh of St Victor, *Didascalicon*, 90.
125 *Quintilian on Education*, xxi.
126 Jerome, 'Letter to Laeta', 371.
127 Augustine, *Confessions*, ii, 2–3.
128 Augustine, *Confessions*, i, 13–14 & iv, 1.
129 Augustine, *Confessions*, iii, 3–6.
130 Augustine, *On Christian Teaching*, 64.

131 Some authors responded directly to this need to reconcile classical works with Christian morals by adapting ancient texts. Pierre Bersuire (also known as Petrus Berchorius) adapted Ovid in this way in his *Ovidius Moralizatus*. See Reynolds, *The 'Ovidius Moralizatus' of Petrus Berchorius*. Meanwhile, Giovanni Dominici utterly denounced the use of such texts within the classroom. Dominici, *On the Education of Children*, 36.

132 Jerome lays out an entire curriculum of reading for Paula. The Psalter was succeeded by Proverbs, Ecclesiastes, Job, the Gospels, the Acts of the Apostles, the Epistles, the Prophets, the Heptateuch, the books of Kings, Chronicles, Ezra, and Esther. Only then was she allowed to read the Song of Songs for 'if she were to read it at the beginning she might be harmed by not perceiving that it as the song of a spiritual bridal expressed in fleshly language': Jerome, *Letter to Laeta*, ch. 12.

133 Philippe of Navarre, *Les Quatre ages*, 9.

134 Dubois, *Recovery of the Holy Land*, 126.

135 Gerson, 'A.B.C. des simples gens', VII, 154–57.

136 Piccolomini, 'The Education of Boys', 163.

137 John of Salisbury, *Metalogicon*, 68.

138 Gerson, 'Pro pueris', IX, 687

139 Piccolomini, 'The Education of Boys', 163.

140 Gerson, 'A.B.C. des simples gens', VII, 154–57.

141 Vincent of Beauvais, *De eruditione*, 58.

142 *Commendation of the Clerk*, 225.

143 Gerson, 'Au précepteur du Dauphin', II, 203–15.

144 Gerson, 'Au précepteur du Dauphin', II, 203.

145 Gerson, 'Au précepteur du Dauphin', II, 212–13.

146 Piccolomini, 'The Education of Boys', 163.

147 Piccolomini, 'The Education of Boys', 209, and Quintilian, *Institutio*, 1.8.v.
148 Piccolomini, 'The Education of Boys', 208–11.
149 Piccolomini, 'The Education of Boys', 214–15.
150 *St. Augustine on Education*, 47.
151 Gerson, 'Au précepteur du Dauphin', VII, 213.
152 Piccolomini, 'The Education of Boys', 216–17.
153 On a side note, Piccolomini himself wrote a feisty *novella*, *De duobus amantibus*, which Rosamund Mitchell describes as 'slight, unedifying, [and] amusing': Mitchell, *The Laurels and the Tiara*, 47–55. Some did have issue with Ovid, and so the *Ovide moralisé* was born in the first half of the fourteenth century.
154 Dominici, *On the Education of Children*, 36.
155 Pseudo-Boethius, *On the Teaching of School*, 124.
156 Vincent of Beauvais, *De eruditione*, 9. This can be directly compared to teaching contracts. For example, when the municipal government of Lyon employed teachers, they were described as 'bon, souffisant et discret' — 'good, able and prudent' or as a 'discrete personne' — 'prudent person'. The character of the master was as important as his qualifications in the real world: Archives municipales de Lyon, CC 385 livre 10, fol. 13 & livre 11, fol. 14^v.
157 Though Pseudo-Boethius does suggest that the teacher should be intelligent but not 'confound the ignorant'. In other words, they should understand their audience. Pseudo-Boethius, *On the Teaching of School*, 124.
158 Dubois, *Recovery of the Holy Land*, 136.
159 Dubois, *Recovery of the Holy Land*, 139.
160 *Commendation of the Clerk*, 216.
161 *Commendation of the Clerk*, 216.

162 *Commendation of the Clerk*, 223.
163 *Commendation of the Clerk*, 223.
164 Gerson, 'Pro pueris', XI, 687.
165 The comportment of the master is paramount in the Pseudo-Boethian recommendations too. There the lone master is seen as representing all masters and any misbehaviour would reflect poorly on the whole profession. Pseudo-Boethius, *On the Teaching of School*, 129.
166 *Augustine on Education*, 338.
167 Gerson, 'Pro pueris', IX, 686.
168 Gerson, 'Pro pueris', IX, 686.
169 Gerson, 'Pro pueris', IX, 687.
170 Gerson, 'Pro pueris', IX, 687.
171 Gerson, 'Pro pueris', IX, 688.
172 Gerson, 'Pro pueris', IX, 688.
173 Gerson, 'Pro pueris', IX, 687.
174 *Commendation of the Clerk*, 215.
175 *Commendation of the Clerk*, 216.
176 *Commendation of the Clerk*, 217.
177 *Commendation of the Clerk*, 217–18.
178 Gerson, 'A.B.C. des simples gens', VII, 154.
179 Quintilian, *Institutio*, 1.1.vi.
180 Barton Tobin, *Vincent of Beauvais*, 143.
181 Vincent of Beauvais, *De eruditione*, 175.
182 Vincent of Beauvais, *De eruditione*, 176.
183 Vincent of Beauvais, *De eruditione*, 178.
184 Jerome, 'Letter to Laeta', pt. 4.
185 Gerson, 'Pro pueris', IX, 688.
186 Piccolomini, 'The Education of Boys', 169.
187 Vincent, *De eruditione*, 177.

188 Piccolomini, *The Education of Boys*, 141. See also Willemsen, *Back to the Schoolyard*, 196–97, for fifteenth-century Italian images of girls learning spinning and needlework while their male counterparts were instructed in reading.

189 Jerome, 'Letter to Laeta', pt. 10.

190 Vincent of Beauvais, *De eruditione*, 178.

191 Jerome, 'Letter to Laeta', pt. 12.

192 Abelard, 'De studio litterarum', ch. 325–36.

193 Barton Tobin, *Vincent of Beauvais*, 32–33.

194 *Du Chevalier de la Tour Landry*, 176–77.

195 From Vincent of Beauvais's *Speculum doctrina* quoted in Gabriel, *Educational Ideas of Vincent of Beauvais*, 16.

196 Vincent of Beauvais, *De eruditione*, 176.

197 *Du Chevalier de la Tour Landry*, 178.

198 Dubois, *Recovery of the Holy Land*, 138.

199 Dubois, *Recovery of the Holy Land*, 119.

200 Dubois, *Recovery of the Holy Land*, 138.

201 Dubois, *Recovery of the Holy Land*, 138–39.

202 Dubois, *Recovery of the Holy Land*, 150–51.

203 Philippe of Navarre, *Les Quatre Ages*, 17.

204 Philippe of Navarre, *Les Quatre Ages*, 16–17.

Bibliography

This bibliography covers not only the texts and histories cited in the above work but also suggestions for further reading.

Archival Sources

Lyon, Archives municipales de Lyon, CC 385 livre 10, fol. 13; and livre 11, fol. 14^v
Vatican, Biblioteca Apostolica Vaticana, Pal. Lat. 1252
Vatican, Biblioteca Apostolica Vaticana, Reg. Lat. 1642

Primary Sources

Abelard, Peter, 'De studio litterarum (Epistola IX)', in *Patrologia Latina*, ed. by Jacques-Paul Migne, 217 vols (Cambridge: Chadwyck-Healey, 1933–), CLXXVIII, 326–36
Ælfric Bata, *Anglo-Saxon Conversations: The Colloquies of Ælfric Bata*, ed. by Scott Gwara, trans. by David W. Porter (Woodbridge: Boydell, 1997)
Anonymous, 'The Commendation of the Clerk', in *University Records and Life in the Middle Ages*, ed.

& trans. by Lynn Thorndike (New York: Columbia University Press, 1944), pp. 201–35

Augustine of Hippo, *St. Augustine on Education*, ed. & trans. by George Howie (South Bend, IN: Gateway, 1969)

——, *The City of God Against the Pagans*, vol. VII (Cambridge, MA: Harvard University Press, 1972)

——, *Confessions*, ed. by James J. O'Donnell, 3 vols (Oxford: Oxford University Press, 1991)

——, *On Christian Teaching*, trans. by R. P. H. Green (Oxford: Oxford University Press, 2008)

Benedict of Nursia, *The Rule of St Benedict*, ed. by William Kemp Lowther Clarke (London: S.P.C.K., 1931)

Pseudo-Boethius, *De disciplina scolarium*, ed. by Olga Weijers (Leiden: Brill, 1976) Chaucer, Geoffrey, *The Canterbury Tales*, trans. by David Wright (Oxford: Oxford University Press, 1985)

Le Chevalier de la Tour Landry, *Du Chevalier de la Tour Landry: Pour l'enseignement de ses filles*, ed. by Anatole de Montaiglon (Paris: Jannet, 1854)

Dominici, Giovanni, *On the Education of Children*, trans. by Arthur Basil Coté (Washington DC: Catholic University of America, 1927)

Dubois, Pierre, *The Recovery of the Holy Land*, ed. & trans. by Walther Brandt (New York: Columbia University Press, 1956)

Froissart, Jean, '*Un Galant de douze ans*', in *Anthologie poétique française: Moyen age II*, ed. by André Mary (Paris: Garnier-Flammarion, 1967), pp. 155–56

Gerson, Jean, *Oeuvres complètes*, ed. by Palemon Glorieux, 10 vols (Paris: Desclée, 1960–73)

Giles of Rome, *Li Livres du gouvernement des rois: A XIIIth Century French Version of Egidio Colonna's Treatise 'De regimine principum'*, ed. by Samuel Paul Molenaer (New York: Columbia University Press, 1899)

Hugh of Saint-Victor, *The Didascalicon of Hugh of St Victor: A Medieval Guide to the Arts*, trans. by Jerome Taylor (New York: Columbia University Press, 1961)

Humanist Educational Treatises, ed. & trans. by Craig W. Kallendorf (Cambridge, MA: Harvard University Press, 2002)

Isidore of Seville, *The Etymologies of Isidore of Seville*, trans. by Stephen A. Barney, W. J. Lewis, J. A. Beach, & Oliver Berghof (Cambridge: Cambridge University Press, 2010)

Jerome, *Select Letters of St. Jerome*, trans. by F. A. Wright (London: William Heinemann, 1933)

John of Salisbury, *The 'Metalogicon' of John of Salisbury: A Twelfth-Century Defence of the Verbal and Logical Arts of the Trivium*, ed. & trans. by Daniel D. McGarry (Berkeley: University of California Press, 1955)

Medieval Grammar and Rhetoric: Language Arts and Literary Theory, AD 300–1475, ed. by Rita Copeland & Ineke Sluiter (Oxford: Oxford University Press, 2009)

Neckham, Alexander, 'A List of Textbooks (From *Sacerdos ad altare*), ca. 1210', in *Medieval Grammar and Rhetoric: Language Arts and Literary Theory, AD 300–1475*, ed. by Rita Copeland & Ineke

Sluiter (Oxford: Oxford University Press, 2009), pp. 531–41

Philippe of Navarre, *Les Quatre ages de l'homme: Traité moral de Philippe de Navarre*, ed. by Marcel Fréville (Paris: Libraire de Firmin Didot, 1888)

Piccolomini, Aeneas Silvius, 'The Education of Boys', in *Humanist Educational Treatises*, ed. & trans. by Craig Kallendorf (Cambridge, MA: Harvard University Press), pp. 127–260

de Pizan, Christine, *The Book of the City of the Ladies*, ed. & trans. by Rosalind Brown-Grant (London: Penguin, 1999)

Quintilian, *The Orator's Education*, ed. & trans. by Donald A. Russell, 5 vols (Cambridge, MA: Harvard University Press, 2001)

Quintilian on Education: Being a Translation of Selected Passages from the 'Institutio oratoria' with an Introductory Essay on Quintilian, his Environment and his Theory of Education, ed. by William Smail (Oxford: Clarendon, 1938)

Les Statuts et privilèges des universités françaises depuis leur fondation jusqu'en 1789, ed. by Marcel Fournier, 4 vols. (Paris: Larose & Forcel, 1890–94; repr. Aalen: Scientia Verlag Aalen, 1970)

Vincent of Beauvais, *De eruditione filiorum nobelium*, ed. by Arpad Steiner (Cambridge, MA: Medieval Academy of America, 1938)

William of Tournai, *The 'De instructione puerorum' of William of Tournai, O.P.*, ed. by James A. Corbett (South Bend, IN: Mediaeval Institute, University of Notre Dame, 1955)

Secondary Sources

Alexandre-Bidon, Danièle, 'La Lettre volée: Apprendre à lire à l'enfant au Moyen Âge', *Annales*, 44 (1989), 953-92

——, & Marie-Thérèse Lorcin, *Système éducatif et cultures dans l'Occident medieval (XIIe-XVe siècle)* (Paris: Orphrys, 1998)

Ariès, Philippe, *Centuries of Childhood*, trans. by Robert Baldick (London: Cape, 1962)

Bailey, Mark, 'Sir John de Wingfield and the Foundation of Wingfield College', in *Wingfield College and its Patrons: Piety and Prestige in Medieval Suffolk*, ed. by Peter Bloore & Edward Martin (Woodbridge: Boydell & Brewer, 2015), pp. 31-48

Barton Tobin, Rosemary, *Vincent of Beauvais' 'De Eruditione filiorum nobilium': The Education of Women* (New York: Peter Lang, 1984)

Begley, Ronald B., & Joseph W. Koterski (eds), *Medieval Education* (New York: Fordham University Press, 2005)

Black, Robert, *Humanism and Education in Medieval and Renaissance Italy: Tradition and Innovation in Latin Schools from the Twelfth to the Fifteenth Century* (Cambridge: Cambridge University Press, 2001)

——, *Education and Society in Florentine Tuscany: Teachers, Pupils and Schools, c. 1250-1500* (Leiden: Brill, 2007)

Bowen, James, *A History of Western Education*, 3 vols (London: Methuen, 1981)

Camargo, Martin, 'Grammar School Rhetoric: The Compedia of John Longe and John Miller', in *Medieval Grammar and the Literary Arts*, ed. by Rita Copeland, David Lawton, & Wendy Scase, New Medieval Literatures, 11 (Turnhout: Brepols, 2009), pp. 91–112

Carruthers, Mary, *The Book of Memory* (Cambridge: Cambridge University Press, 1990)

Clanchy, Michael T., *From Memory to Written Record: England, 1066–1307*, 3rd edn (Oxford: Blackwell, 2013)

Cribiore, Gabriella, *Gymnastics of the Mind: Greek Education in Hellenistic and Roman Egypt* (Princeton: Princeton University Press, 2001)

Deschaux, Robert, 'Eloy d'Amerval et l'éducation des enfants', in *L'Enfant au Moyen-Age: Littérature et civilisation. Senefiance no. 9* (Aix-en-Provence: CUER MA Université de Provence, 1980), pp. 375–88

Dumitrescu, Irina A., 'The Grammar of Pain in Ælfric Bata's *Colloquies*', *Forum for Modern Language Studies*, 45, no. 3 (2009), 239–53

Fijałkowski, Adam, 'The Education of Women in the Works of Vincent of Beauvais, OP (†1264)', in *Geistesleben im 13. Jahrhundert*, ed. by Jan A. Aertsen & Andreas Speer (Berlin: Walter de Gruyter, 2000), pp. 513–26

Gabriel, Astrik, *The Educational Ideas of Vincent of Beauvais* (South Bend, IN: Mediaeval Institute, University of Notre Dame, 1956)

Gehl, Paul F., *A Moral Art: Grammar, Society and Culture in Trecento Florence* (Ithaca, NY: Cornell University Press, 1993)

Grendler, Paul F., *Schooling in Renaissance Italy: Literacy and Learning, 1300–1600* (Baltimore: Johns Hopkins University Press, 1989)

Guilbert, Sylvette, 'Les Écoles rurales en Champagne au XVe siècle: Enseignement et promotion sociale', *Annales de l'Est*, 34 (1982), 127–47

Hanawalt, Barbara, *Growing up in Medieval London: The Experience of Childhood in History* (Oxford: Oxford University Press, 1993)

Haskins, Charles Homer, 'The Life of Medieval Students as Illustrated by their Letters', *The American Historical Review*, 3 (1898), 203–29 (repr. in Charles Homer Haskins, *Studies in Mediaeval Culture* (Oxford: Clarendon, 1929), pp. 1–35)

——, 'A List of Text-Books from the Close of the Twelfth Century', *Harvard Studies in Classical Philology*, 20 (1909), 75–94

Hunt, R. W., *The History of Grammar in the Middle Ages: Collected Papers*, ed. by G. L. Bursill-Hall (Amsterdam: John Benjamins, 1980)

Huppert, Georges, *Public Schools in Renaissance France* (Urbana, IL: University of Illinois Press, 1984)

de Jong, Mayke, *In Samuel's Image: Child Oblation in the Early Medieval West* (Leiden: Brill, 1996)

Jongenelen, Bas, & Parsons, Ben, 'The Virtuous Life in Jan van Boendale's *Der Leken Spieghel* (The Layman's Mirror)', *The Bartholomeus Society for*

Medieval Studies (2008) <http://www.bsms.nl/pub_en.html> [accessed 6 July 2013]

Kagan, Richard L., *Students and Society in Early Modern Spain* (Baltimore: Johns Hopkins University Press, 1974)

Lanham, Carol D. (ed.), *Latin Grammar and Rhetoric: From Classical Theory to Medieval Practice* (London: Continuum Books, 2003)

Leach, Arthur F., *English Schools at the Reformation, 1546–1548* (Westminster: Constable, 1896)

——, *Educational Charters and Document, 598–1909* (Cambridge: Cambridge University Press, 1911)

——, *The Schools of Medieval England* (London: Methuen, 1915)

Lynch, Sarah B., 'Christine de Pizan and Education in the Middle Ages', *The History Review, University College Dublin*, 16 (2006), 95–112

——, 'The Children's Cloister: Choirboys and Space in Late-Medieval Cathedrals', *Bulletin for International Medieval Research*, 19 (2013), 44–61

——, 'Pupils and Sources in Late Medieval Lyon', *Espacio, Tiempo y Educación*, 2, no. 2 (2015)

——, *Elementary and Grammar Education in Late Medieval France: Lyon, 1285–1530* (Amsterdam: Amsterdam University Press, 2017)

McCullough, David, *John Adams* (New York: Simon & Schuster, 2001)

McGarry, Daniel D., 'Educational Theory in the *Metalogicon* of John of Salisbury', *Speculum*, 23 (1948), 659–75

Mehl, Jean-Michel, *Les Jeux au royaume de France au XIIIe au début du XVIe siècle* (Paris: Fayard, 1990)

Mitchell, Rosamond J., *The Laurels and the Tiara: Pope Pius II (1458-1464)* (London: Harvill, 1962)

Moran Cruz, Jo Ann Hoeppner, 'Literacy and Education in Northern England, 1350-1530: A Methodological Inquiry', *Northern History*, 17 (1981), 1-23

——, *The Growth of English Schooling 1340-1548: Learning, Literacy, and Laicisation in Pre-Reformation York Diocese* (Princeton: Princeton University Press, 1985)

——, 'England: Education and Society', in *A Companion to Britain in the Late Middle Ages*, ed. by Stephen Rigby (Oxford: Blackwell, 2003), pp. 451-71

Mulchahey, M. Michèle, *'First the Bow is Bent in Study...': Dominican Education before 1350* (Toronto: Pontifical Institute of Mediaeval Studies, 1998)

Murphy, James J., *Rhetoric in the Middle Ages: A History of the Rhetorical Theory from St Augustine to the Renaissance* (Berkeley: University of California Press, 1998)

Orme, Nicholas, *English Schools in the Middle Ages* (London: Methuen, 1973)

——, 'The Education of the Courtier', in *English Court Culture in the Later Middle Ages*, ed. by V. J. Scattergood & J. W. Sherbourne (London: Duckworth, 1983), pp. 63-85

——, *From Childhood to Chivalry: The Education of English Kings and Aristocracy, 1066-1530* (London: Methuen, 1984)

―――, *Medieval Children* (New Haven: Yale University Press, 2003)

―――, 'Education and Recreation', in *Late Medieval England*, ed. by Raluca Radulescu & Alison Truelove (Manchester: Manchester University Press, 2005), pp. 63–83

―――, *Medieval Schools: From Roman Britain to Renaissance England* (New Haven: Yale University Press, 2006)

―――, *English School Exercises, 1420–1530* (Turnhout: Brepols, 2013)

―――, 'Games and Education in Late Medieval England', in *Games and Gaming in Medieval Literature*, ed. by Serina Patterson (New York: Palgrave MacMillian, 2015), pp. 45–60

Parry, A. W., *Education in England in the Middle Ages* (London: University Tutorial Press, 1920)

Parsons, Ben, 'The Way of the Road: The Functions of Beating in Late Medieval Pedagogy', *Modern Philology*, 113, no. 1 (2015), 1–26

Petersen, Joan M., 'The Education of Girls in Fourth-Century Rome', in *The Church and Childhood. Studies in Church History 31*, ed. by Diana Wood (Oxford: Blackwell for the Ecclesiastical History Society, 1994), pp. 29–37

Planchart, Alejandro Enrique, 'The Early Career of Guillaume Du Fay', *Journal of the American Musicology Society*, 46, no. 3 (1993), 341–68

Planche, Alice, 'Culture et contre-culture dans *L'Epinette amoureuse* de Jean Froissart: les écoles et les jeux', in *L'Enfant au Moyen-Age: Littérature et civilisation. Senefiance no. 9* (Aix-en-Provence: CUER MA Université de Provence, 1980), pp. 389–403

de Pommerol, Marie-Henriette Jullien, 'Livres d'étudiants, bibliothèques de collèges et d'universités', in *Histoire des bibliothèques françaises: Les Bibliothèques médiévales du VIe siècle à 1530*, ed. by André Vernet (Paris: Promodis, 1989), pp. 93–94

Rashdall, Hastings, *The Universities of Europe in the Middle Ages*, 2nd edn, rev. by A. B. Emden & F. M. Powicke, 3 vols (Oxford: Clarendon, 1936)

Reynolds, Suzanne, *Medieval Reading: Grammar, Rhetoric, and the Classical Text* (Cambridge: Cambridge University Press, 1996)

Reynolds, William Donald, 'The "Ovidius Moralizatus" of Petrus Berchorius: An Introduction and Translation' (unpublished doctoral dissertation, University of Illinois at Urbana-Champagne, 1971)

Riché, Pierre, *Education and Culture in the Barbarian West from the Sixth through Eighth Century*, trans. by John J. Contreni (Columbia, SC: University of South Carolina Press, 1976)

——, *Éducation et culture dans l'Occident médiéval* (Aldershot: Variorum, 1993)

de Ridder-Symoens, Hilde, 'Education and Literacy in the Burgundian-Habsburg Netherlands', *Canadian Journal of Netherlandic Studies*, 16–1 (1995), 6–21

Schedel, Hartmann, *Liber chronicarum*, trans. by Georg Alt (Nuremberg: Anton Koberger, 1493)

Searle, Ronald, *The Terrors of St Trinian's and Other Drawings* (London: Penguin, 2006)

Shahar, Shulamith, *Childhood in the Middle Ages* (London: Routledge, 1990)

Sheffler, David L., *Schools and Schooling in Late Medieval Germany: Regensburg, 1250–1500* (Leiden: Brill, 2008)

Thorndike, Lynn, 'Elementary and Secondary Education in the Middle Ages', *Speculum*, 15 (1940), 400–08

——, *University Records and Life in the Middle Ages* (New York: Columbia University Press, 1949)

Willans, Geoffrey, & Ronal Searle, *Molesworth* (London: Penguin, 2000)

Willemsen, Annemarieke, *Back to the Schoolyard: The Daily Practice of Medieval and Renaissance Education*, Studies in European Urban History 1100–1800, 15 (Turnhout: Brepols, 2008)

Woolf, Alex, *Medieval Realms: Education* (San Diego: Lucent, 2004)

Credits

Cover created by Kısmet Press from: 1) Spitz Master, The Four Evangelists. Ink on parchment, ca.1420. Los Angeles, The J. Paul Getty Museum, lido.getty.edu-gm-obj110501. <https://commons.wikimedia.org/wiki/File:Spitz_Master_(French,_active_about_1415_-_1425)_-_The_Four_Evangelists_-_Google_Art_Project.jpg>; <https://www.getty.edu/art/collection/objects/103429/spitz-master-the-four-evangelists-french-about-1420/>; 2) Master of Anthony of Burgundy, Miniature des quatre évangélistes extraite des Heures noires de Galeazzo Maria Sforza. Illumination on parchment, 15th century. Vienna, Österreichische Nationalbibliothek, Codex Vindobo, MS 1856, fol.32^v. <https://commons.wikimedia.org/wiki/File:Sforza_Black_hours_-_%C3%96NB_Cod1856_f32v_-_four_evangelists.jpg>. Original images in the public domain, edited by Kısmet Press, and republished under the same license.

Throughout the Middle Ages, great intellectuals from Jerome to Jean Gerson all commented on education. What was its purpose? What practices best achieved the intended aims? This volume introduces the central themes that ran through literature on education, from its fixation on moral instruction to recommendations on playtime. It explores writing from the first century to the educational treatises of Renaissance Italy and discusses the important place that education, even of small children, held in medieval thought.

Dr Sarah B. Lynch is an assistant professor at Angelo State University, Texas. A graduate of University College Dublin, Trinity College Dublin, and the University of Leeds, she specializes in the history of elementary and grammar education in the later Middle Ages. Her doctoral thesis, concentrating on schools, teachers, and pupils in late-medieval Lyon, was published by Amsterdam University Press in 2017. She received the Olivia Remie Constable Award from the Medieval Academy of America in 2018 for her ongoing project on educational legacies in medieval French wills.

www.ingramcontent.com/pod-product-compliance
Lightning Source LLC
Chambersburg PA
CBHW071347080526
44587CB00017B/3000